Charles Seale-Hayne Library
University of Plymouth
(01752) 588 588
LibraryandITenquiries@plymouth.ac.uk

MEDICINE, LAW AND SOCIAL CHANGE

Titles in the series:

A Patient's Right to Know: Information, Disclosure, the Doctor and the Law
Sheila A.M. McLean, University of Glasgow

New Reproductive Techniques: A Legal Perspective
Douglas J. Cusine, University of Aberdeen

Medico-Legal Aspects of Reproduction and Parenthood
J.K. Mason, University of Edinburgh

Law Reform and Human Reproduction
Edited by *Sheila A.M. McLean*, University of Glasgow

Legal and Ethical Issues in the Management of the Dementing Elderly
Mary Gilhooly, University of Glasgow

Legal Issues in Human Reproduction
Edited by *Sheila A.M. McLean*, University of Glasgow

Mental Illness: Prejudice, Discrimination and the Law
Tom Campbell, Australian National University, Canberra and *Chris Heginbotham*, King's Fund College, London

Pharmaceuticals in the European Community
Ken Collins, Member of the European Parliament and *Sheila A.M. McLean*, University of Glasgow

Pregnancy at Work
Noreen Burrows, University of Glasgow

Changing People: The Law and Ethics of Behaviour Modification
Alexander McCall Smith, University of Edinburgh

Health Resources and the Law: Who Gets What and Why
Robert G. Lee, Wilde Sapte and *Frances H. Miller*, University of Boston

Surrogacy and the Moral Economy
Derek Morgan, University College, Swansea

Family Planning Practice and the Law
Kenneth McK. Norrie, University of Aberdeen

Mental Health Law in Context: Doctors' Orders?
Michael Cavadino, University of Sheffield

Artificial Reproduction and Reproductive Rights
Athena Liu, University of Hong Kong

Abortion Regimes
Kerry Petersen, La Trobe University

All titles are provisional

MEDICINE, LAW AND SOCIAL CHANGE

The Impact of Bioethics, Feminism and Rights
Movements on Medical Decision-Making

LEANNA DARVALL
La Trobe University

Dartmouth
Aldershot · Brookfield USA · Hong Kong · Singapore · Sydney

Published by
Dartmouth Publishing Company Limited
Gower House
Croft Road
Aldershot
Hants GU11 3HR
England

Dartmouth Publishing Company
Old Post Road
Brookfield
Vermont 05036
USA

A CIP catalogue record for this book is available from the British Library

ISBN 1 85521 077 0
Printed and Bound in Great Britain by
Hartnolls Limited, Bodmin, Cornwall.

To the memory of my parents

ʋ

Contents

Preface

This book is about medical decision-making. In particular, it concerns medical and legal attitudes to changing social views of patients' involvement in decisions affecting their bodies. Until relatively recently, there was widespread acceptance of a paternalistic model of medical care. Grounded in the Hippocratic tradition, this model vests doctors with a responsibility to care for patients. This responsibility includes making decisions in a patient's best interests, whether or not such decisions accord with the patient's own values and preferences.

Professional justification for medical paternalism includes the notion that technical expertise is of fundamental importance in medical decision-making.[1] The following comment of Sir Raymond Hoffenberg, President of the British College of Physicians illustrates this view:

> My concern to preserve the central role of the doctor in clinical decisions, moral or otherwise, is not a reflexion of professional self-interest or a wish to perpetuate professional sovereignty. It is based on my belief that such decisions must rest on a proper knowledge of all the medical consequences of each option, physical and psychological, qualitative as well as quantitative; that they must be made with critical and professional detachment; and that they should be conveyed to and discussed with the patient and the family with compassion and sensitivity. This combination of qualities, I believe, is best embodied in the well-trained doctor, and the interests of patients will best be served by their proper application. In the words of Franz Ingelfinger "If you agree that the physician's primary function is to make the patient feel better, a certain amount of authoritarianism, paternalism, and domination are the essence of the physician's effectiveness".[2]

1

From the sixties onwards, there was no longer unquestioning public acceptance of medical paternalism in either Australia or the United States. Prevailing anti-authoritarian sentiments prompted changes in attitudes towards the medical profession. In the United States, changing social values concerning all forms of authority crystallized into social movements whose origins can be traced to the American civil rights movement. Although losing its momentum as a protest movement during the seventies, this movement nevertheless paved the way for interest groups to develop individual rights' agendas.[3] Stephen Toulmin characterizes this period as an era of 'adversary politics' in which the goals of political action were defined in group rather than national terms. Such a state of affairs, he argues, contributed to the undermining of public trust in both professional and institutional authority.[4] Similar interest groups and movements began emerging in Australia from the late sixties onwards. During the following decades, these groups developed health agendas in response to a series of medical disasters, changes in health care delivery and a rapidly developing medical technology.

The thalidomide and diethylstilboestrol (DES) drug tragedies and unethical human subject research practices in the United States focused national and international attention on the medical research establishment. Technological developments relating to organ transplantation, the new reproductive technologies, genetic engineering and life-support systems ensured an ongoing public interest in the medical profession. At the same time, scholars, interest groups, courts and legislatures grappled with legal and ethical issues concerning the application of the new medical technologies. Contemporaneous changes in the delivery of health care services significantly affected the doctor-patient relationship. The demise of solo practitioners and an increase in group practice meant that patients were less likely to be regularly attended to by the same doctor. This was in stark contrast to the long-standing associations formed between family practitioners of the past and their patients. Developments in medical technology caused increasing specialization which has particularly affected hospitalized patients. For this group, team treatment by specialists and technicians generally precludes the possibility of an established, continuous relationship with the same doctor.[5] In Australia, privately insured patients fare much better in this regard. This is because private insurance entitles patients, whether in public or private hospitals, to a specialist of their choice. Whilst choice in this instance will usually be made by a patient's general practitioner, the practical outcome of private insurance is that a particular doctor assumes responsibility for a patient's treatment and well being. By and large, the effect of these structural changes has been to create a relationship between doctors and patients most aptly described as one between strangers. In turn, this appears to have encouraged American (and to a far lesser extent Australian) patients, to seek legal redress for injuries resulting from medical negligence, including failure to disclose information.

The discrepancy between the rates of malpractice litigation in America and Australia is attributable to a number of factors. From the early seventies on, the American legal profession encouraged the involvement of civil rights lawyers in medical issues. In particular, they were urged to participate in framing biomedical legislation and in scrutinizing medical decisions to ensure that human rights were not subordinated to the interests of medical progress.[6] In the United States, the contingent fee system provides American patients with a strong incentive to litigate. In contrast, restrictive procedural rules, as well as rules regarding costs, operate as a significant deterrent to litigation in Australia. In addition, the receptive attitude of American courts to professional disclosure obligations throughout the early seventies no doubt encouraged potential litigants.[7]

In both Australia and the United States, the anti-authoritarian mood of the times found expression in rights and autonomy-based arguments. When applied in a medical context, these perspectives directly challenged medical paternalism. According to certain theoretical views, a practitioner's responsibility to patients derives from, and is limited by, the principle of respect for self-determination.[8] Such a principle is valued for its own sake, rather than because it enhances patient health or welfare. Various liberation movements sought to expose the partiality of legal, political, social and cultural norms. which were perceived as products of historically situated individuals with particular race, class, gender, biases and interests.[9] The common law was also criticized on the grounds that it endorsed professional standards thereby recognizing professional autonomy at the expense of patients' autonomy and rights. Feminists argued that medical knowledge and practice were imbued with sexist prejudice and that women were excluded from decision-making, either as patients or health care professionals. To rectify this situation, they devised theories and strategies which enhanced patient autonomy and rights.

Rights and autonomy-based arguments were by no means universally accepted. Certain moral theologians and philosophers, amongst others, regarded these perspectives as particularly inappropriate for the doctor-patient relationship because they threatened trust and because they failed to take sufficient account of the interdependence of both parties. Cultural feminists argued that an ethics of rights provided an inadequate moral framework as it failed to incorporate the subjective experiences of individuals in particular contexts. Alternative ethical frameworks including those based on an ethics of virtue and an ethics of care were developed in order to redress these perceived shortcomings. By the mid-eighties, the emphasis on autonomy was being queried in bioethical circles. Whilst acknowledging the importance of this concept in countering the excesses of medical paternalism, it was nevertheless argued that an undue emphasis on individualism is likely to lead to patient isolation and abandonment. It was also perceived as a threat to the notion of community. Just as thoughts of this nature were being aired, the AIDS epidemic occurred. The demands of AIDS activists and gay rights groups for community consultation and rights of access to unapproved drugs challenged a number of fundamental assumptions of human subject research and regulatory policy. At the same time, they re-kindled tensions between individual rights and community interest in health issues.

This narrative discusses law and medicine in a social context. Its central theme is the interaction of social forces and processes of social change, with particular reference to the role of law as it affects medical decision-making. Three major forces of social change, consumerism, feminism and bioethics are described in Chapter One. An additional force, the gay rights movement, is introduced in Chapter Five. The reader should bear in mind that these movements are not homogenous entities and that each is composed of diverse groups with distinct and frequently different perspectives. As a result, the views presented throughout are those of particular individuals and as such, are not necessarily representative. It is equally important to appreciate that certain values and concepts are shared by a broad spectrum of individuals and groups.

So it is that certain philosophers, lawyers, doctors, radical feminists and gay rights activists embrace an autonomy perspective, whilst some moral theologians and cultural feminists espouse an ethics of care. These unlikely theoretical liaisons make classification a difficult and somewhat arbitrary process. Consequently, whilst certain views are described as legal, or medical, they might just as easily have been identified as feminist, and vice versa. The reader should also note that, despite particular theoretical perspectives having been identified at the outset, each of these perspectives is not necessarily referred to in every section of the text. Such omissions occur largely because some perspectives are capable of dual classification. So for example, in Chapter Three, discussions of an ethics of care are classified as legal or medical rather than feminist. The relevance of a cultural feminist perspective may nevertheless be assumed by virtue of its recognition of a commonly held concept and the analytical tools which it has developed therefrom.

Whilst writing this book, I was acutely aware that an entire volume could, indeed should, be devoted to each of the social forces which are touched upon so briefly. I also realized that its selective approach does not do justice to the comprehensive range of medical perspectives on particular issues. Despite these limitations, this book informs readers about a number of major ideas in the health debate and their influence on clinical and research decison-making in Australia. Because bioethics and various social movements which have influenced the health debate originated in America, it seemed important to trace the extent of their influence on law regulating medical decision-making in that country as well as in Australia.

The task of selecting particular bioethical issues to illustrate changes in decision-making processes was not an easy one. Informed consent was chosen because it emerged as arguably the most widely debated issue of the eighties, both in Australia and overseas. Refusal of medical treatment was included because of widespread public interest in this topic both in America and Australia and because it resulted in unique legislation in one Australian State. Dramatic challenges to the decision-making processes of Australian and American regulatory authorities, largely as a result of the AIDS crisis, made human subject research an inevitable choice. Each of these areas focuses on decision-making by competent individuals. In the area of refusal of medical treatment, decision-making by incompetent patients is also included because the major thrust of the debate concerns this category of patients.

The desire to undertake this project arose from a long-standing interest in medico-legal issues and from my teaching in Torts, Consumer Protection, and Law and Medical Ethics. The catalyst to begin writing was undoubtedly Steven Toulmin's eloquent talk on the origins and development of bioethics in the United States, at the New York Academy of Sciences meeting in May 1989. My ideas and information were gleaned from many books and articles. In particular, **A History and Theory of Informed Consent** by Ruth Faden and Tom Beauchamp provided an inspirational model.

Throughout this endeavour I have received generous assistance from my family, friends and colleagues. In particular, I wish to thank Dr Martin Chanock, who was the personification of the discerning reader on the proverbial Clapham omnibus, in relation to various drafts of the manuscript. I also wish to express my gratitude to Dr Grisha Sklovsky who cast an experienced and critical eye over each chapter. I am also grateful to Dr Jason Parker for his insightful comments. My thanks are also due to Dr

Ken Harvey, who kindly agreed to read Chapter Two, to Peter Heffey and Professor Harold Luntz for their comments in relation to Chapter Three and to John Willis, Chris Corns and Dr Helga Kuhse for their advice concerning Chapter Four. I am also indebted to Professor Sheila McLean for her constructive comments, criticisms and editorial advice and for the fruitful discussions that we had together during my visit to Glasgow.

While writing this book I spent two weeks as a visiting fellow at the Hastings Center in New York, where the atmosphere was extraordinarily conducive to innovative thinking and scholarship. My thanks to Daniel Callahan, who somehow found the time to give me the benefit of his comments on Chapter One. I am also extremely grateful to Marna Howarth, the Center's librarian, who never failed to locate valuable source materials. Keeping abreast of overseas developments is a problem familiar to Australian researchers; I am particularly indebted to Hellen Gellband, Office of Technology, Washington D.C., for providing me so promptly with reports.

If a 'but for' test were to be applied to this undertaking, I would have to conclude that 'but for' the skilled advice of Bob Powell and Beverly Tannock, who introduced me to the wonders of word-processing, this book could not have been completed within the publisher's time-frame. I am also grateful to Sue Stoikos, Denise Lumsden and Melissa Fisher for their willing and expert administrative assistance. Credit is also due to Lesley Vick for her painstaking efforts in proof-reading my manuscript. Profound thanks are due to my good friend Bette Moore, not only for her perceptive editorial skills and insights, but also for her constant support and encouragement. Above all, I am indebted to my family who will undoubtedly breath a collective sigh of relief now that this venture is finally at an end.

Leanna Darvall
La Trobe University
September, 1992

Notes

1. Hoffenberg Sir Raymond., Clinical Freedom. The Nuffield Provincial Hospitals Trust.1987. 72. In contrast, Sir Raymond suggests that lay review of medical research is acceptable to the profession. Id.52.
2. Id.72.
3. Starr P., The Social Transformation of American Medicine. Basic Books Inc. New York 1982, 388.
4. Toulmin S., Divided Loyalties and Ambiguous Relationships. 23 Social Science and Medicine 1986, 783-787.
5. On the nature and effects of team care see Pellegrino E., Protection of Patients' Rights and the Doctor-Patient Relationship. 4 Preventive Medicine 1975, 398.
6. Annas G.J., Medical Remedies and Human Rights: Why Civil Rights Lawyers Must Become Involved in Medical Decision-Making. 2 Human Rights 1972,151,166-7.
7. Danzon P.M., The Frequency and Severity of Medical Malpractice Claims. 27 Journal of Law and Economics 1984, 115, 137 as cited in Trebilcock M.J., Dewees D.N. and Duff D.G., The Medical Malpractice Explosion: An Empirical Assessment of Trends, Determinants and Impacts. 17 Melbourne University Law Review 1990, 539, 548
8. Beauchamp T., The Promise of the Beneficence Model for Medical Ethics. 6 Journal of Contemporary Health Law and Policy 1990, 145, 149.
9. Bordo S., Feminism, Postmodernism, and Gender-Scepticism, in Feminism/Postmodernism. Nicholson L.(ed.), Routledge 1990,133,137-8.

1   The Forces of Change

INTRODUCTION

During the last three decades, the Australian and American medical professions have come under increasing public scrutiny. No longer prepared to tolerate a paternalistic medical system in which patients were excluded from decision-making processes, feminists, consumer groups, bioethicists and others set about reconstructing the clinical relationship so as to provide patients with a decision-making role. The new health rights movements went beyond traditional demands for more medical care by challenging the distribution of power and expertise between doctors and their patients.[1] Paul Starr contends that the intellectual shift in attitude which has occurred is symptomatic of "a deepening ambivalence about medicine in the entire society".[2] Such ambivalence manifests itself in Americans retaining confidence in their own practitioners whilst becoming more hostile towards the profession in general. It is also illustrated by the consumer and women's movements simultaneously claiming "rights of access to and rights of protection against medical authority".[3]

Starr's comments are equally applicable in an Australian context.[4] By the close of the eighties however, a new militancy had emerged amongst gay rights activists and people with AIDS (PWAs). Devoid of the ambivalence which Starr identifies with the consumer and women's movements, the demands of this group are almost exclusively concerned with rights of access and participation. Rejecting rights of protection as paternalistic, AIDS-driven health activism represents a powerful challenge to the traditional assumptions underpinning clinical research. The involvement of the consumer and women's movements and bioethics in health issues and their contributions to public discourse in both Australia and the United States are outlined in the following sections. In Chapter Five, the role of the gay rights movement in shaping regulatory policy is discussed in the context of the AIDS crisis.

THE CONSUMER MOVEMENT

Consumerism, which emerged as a social movement in the United States during the sixties, has been described as representing "an approach of doubt and caution, rather than faith and trust, in any transaction, including the medical"[5]. As a result of modern marketing of technologically sophisticated products and the use of standard form contracts excluding the seller's liability, parties were no longer equal in terms of knowledge and negotiating power. In an effort to ensure informed choice, the consumer movement argued for legislative regulation of consumer transactions for goods and services. A charter of consumer rights, endorsed by the late President Kennedy, included, amongst other things, rights to information and safety. Many of these rights were subsequently incorporated in Federal legislative standards.

The thalidomide drug tragedy directed the attention of the international and national consumer movements to health and safety issues. The promotional practices of the Pharmaceutical Industry and their effect on physicians' prescribing patterns and consumer health were of particular concern. The Federal Food Drug and Cosmetic Act (1938) was amended in 1962 largely in response to the thalidomide disaster. The amendments gave the Federal Food and Drug Administration (FDA) power to refuse marketing approval for any drug not proven safe or effective for use under the conditions prescribed, recommended or suggested in its labelling. Detailed regulations also prescribed the form and content of promotional materials. These amendments were welcomed by the consumer movement as appropriate measures in the interests of public health and welfare.

An important goal of the consumer movement was to secure participation in government decision-making. In the early seventies, the FDA established an advisory committee system which included scientific, industry and consumer representatives. In establishing this system, government acknowledged that prescription drug risk-benefit evaluation should no longer be exclusively undertaken by scientific experts.[6] This trend was to continue. In 1974, Federal regulations required non-medical members to be included on human subject experimentation research ethics committees.[7] In the same year, the role of the doctor as sole decision-maker was challenged in relation to the treatment of handicapped neonates.[8]

Medical consumerism developed a rights agenda derived from both the consumer and the welfare rights movements. This strategy appears to have been prompted in part by technological and organizational changes which occurred in medical practice during the seventies. Increasing specialization, the demise of the solo practitioner, and the corresponding rise of group practice, reduced the likelihood of patients establishing a continuing relationship with a particular practitioner.[9] The application of medical technology, which frequently requires the skills of various medical specialists, altered traditional patterns of interaction between doctors and their patients. The rapid expansion of this technology increased the gap between the parties, both in terms of knowledge and expertise. The resulting patient distrust and alienation, aided and abetted by rights rhetoric, gave rise to the articulation of specific rights and demands for professional accountability and participatory decision-making.

The drafting of a statement of patients'rights by the National Welfare Rights Organization in 1970 has been described as the genesis of the patients' rights movement.[10] In 1973, the American Hospitals Association published "A Patient's Bill of Rights" which included rights in relation to diagnosis and treatment information, the refusal of treatment, confidentiality of information, and privacy. Similar documents were drafted by both patient and provider groups during the decade. Whilst some were subsequently enacted as legislation, others served as voluntary guidelines for acceptable medical conduct.[11]

A similar pattern emerged in Australia where medical consumerism evolved as part of the agenda of consumer, community and special-interest groups.[12] A number of Consumer Associations in Health Services were established during the seventies. Two of these bodies drafted a charter of patients' rights and responsibilities which included a right to be informed in lay terms of a diagnosis and proposed treatment, a right to have such information kept confidential, and a right to refuse treatment.[13] Recently, a comprehensive statement of ethical principles and legal rights has been drafted by the Consumers' Health Forum of Australia with a view to national implementation.[14]

The emergence of patients' rights signalled a significant departure from a medical model of health care based on traditional Hippocratic benevolence.[15] Professional ethical codes emphasising practitioner obligations and virtues, had engendered patient trust and encouraged paternalistic or authoritarian ethics. Demands that patients be incorporated into the decision-making process, with due recognition of their right to make the final decision, provided a significant challenge to the traditional model of medical decision-making.[16] The common law allocation of rights and duties between doctors and patients was equally at odds with newly emerging rights perspectives. In particular, the negligence model was found wanting on the grounds that it endorsed professional autonomy at the expense of patient autonomy and rights.

Rights rhetoric provoked a variety of responses. For some, the language of rights imposed an adversarial framework on the clinical relationship threatening the trust between doctor and patient.[17] For others, this new model of decision-making offered the possibility of a mutually beneficial pooling of knowledge and resources between the parties.[18] David Rothman suggests that declarations of patients' rights had some impact on American practitioners' disclosure practices. By the close of the seventies, he believes that "a small revolution had been effected" in this regard.[19] It should be noted however, that during this period, the doctrine of informed consent was emerging from the American common law. The receptive attitude of the American courts to practitioner disclosure requirements during the early seventies, together with a dramatic increase in malpractice suits, may also explain changes in the attitude and practices of American physicians.

THE WOMEN'S MOVEMENT

The women's movement - one of the most important movements to emerge during the past three decades - is concerned with the social, economic, and political status of women. Feminism, the political arm of this movement, is described as being "not a 'natural' excretion of [woman's] experience but a controversial political interpretation and struggle, by no means universal to women".[20]

Feminists argue that women are stereotyped as incapable of decision-making because of a pervasive system of male domination. From a feminist perspective, male dominance is not limited to the notion of control by individual males, but includes a system of power relationships which works to the advantage of men rather than women.[21] In a medical context, male domination is interwoven with professional dominance.[22] Consequently, the medical profession is regarded as an extended patriarchy reinforcing male dominance in society at large.[23] Increasing the number of female medical practitioners would not automatically alter power imbalances, as some women will inevitably be socialized by the profession into thinking and acting as their male counterparts. Instead, women must be encouraged to take responsibility for decisions concerning their bodies. In addition, there is a need for health services dictated by women's needs and priorities.[24]

The term 'feminist' is frequently used by way of generic description, despite the fact that modern feminist theory has not evolved as a coherent whole, but rather as a number of distinct streams. Of these, liberal, cultural, and radical feminism are discussed in the following text.[25] During the sixties, feminism adopted a rights perspective in keeping with the political mood of the times. In order to minimize the differences between the sexes, liberal feminists demanded that men and women be treated equally by law. In particular, they sought equal rights for women in education and employment.

Intrusion of government and courts into areas regarded as essentially private prompted a reappraisal of the appropriateness of a rights perspective in feminist theory. In response to a balancing of foetal rights against a woman's right to make decisions in the context of abortion, feminists argue that women must be solely responsible for decisions concerning their reproductive choices. Developments in neo-natal care affecting the ability of a foetus to survive outside the womb at increasingly earlier stages and legal recognition of foetal rights, are perceived by many feminists as particularly threatening to women's autonomy. In some American jurisdictions, a consideration of foetal rights has resulted in orders for caesarean sections against the wishes of the women concerned.[26]

One such case, involved a twenty-seven year old married woman (A.C.) in whom a lung tumour was discovered when she was twenty-five weeks pregnant. As her condition was terminal, the issue arose as to what to do about the continuation of her pregnancy. Her doctors believed that foetal viability would be greatly increased if delivery were to occur at twenty-eight weeks. Evidence from her doctor indicated that she was agreeable to having the baby at twenty-eight weeks. In fact, A.C. agreed to palliative treatment both to prolong her life for at least another two weeks and to maintain her own comfort. However, there was no evidence as to what her choice would be prior to twenty-eight weeks. At the time the hospital authorities sought an order to perform a caesarian section, A.C. was heavily sedated.

The trial court held that the twenty-six and one half week foetus was viable and had a fifty to sixty per cent chance of survival if a caesarian section were to be performed as soon as possible. It further held that the State has an important and legitimate interest in protecting potential human life. The court stated that it was unable to determine A.C's present views as to whether the foetus should live or die and ordered the caesarian section to be performed.

10

In refusing to grant a stay on the court order, the District of Columbia Court of Appeals found a protectable legal interest in the life of a viable foetus and confirmed the trial court order.[27] The operation was performed in conformity with the order. The foetus died within two hours of delivery and A.C. two days later.[28]

This and similar decisions have aroused concern because of their effect on women's autonomy. As Janet Gallagher observes:

> The ... 'fetal rights' cases possess great symbolic and precedential significance, but they have less to do with the status of the fetus than with the moral and legal status of women. They reinforce deep societal stereotypes of women, particularly of pregnant women, as somehow incompetent to make moral decisions. They also serve to legitimize a forceful, even physically violent, assertion of doctors' control over pregnancy and childbirth.[29]

Others argue that although recognition of women's autonomy may result in tragedy in the individual case, this is an acceptable cost as "on a broader societal scale, preventing these tragedies comes at the cost of embracing an unprecedented and problematic tyranny of medicine and technology...".[30]

The District of Columbia Court of Appeals subsequently reversed its decision in the case In Re A.C. The court stated that in all such cases a patient's informed choice will be decisive.[31] When a patient is incompetent, a substituted judgement procedure must be adopted to ascertain her wishes. While not completely foreclosing the possibility that a conflicting State interest might be so compelling as to override a patient's wishes, the court nevertheless suggested that such cases were likely to be both rare and exceptional.[32]

Cultural and radical feminism are concerned with differences between women and men in terms of women's potential for physical, psychological, emotional, and material connection with others.[33] Cultural feminists contend that women are more caring and responsible towards others and are capable of a greater degree of physical and psychic intimacy than men.[34] Carol Gilligan argues that women's experience of intimate relationships affects their moral development.[35] Women's moral development is linked with nurture, care, responsibility and relationships, focusing on the particular needs of others. Connection and relationships are incorporated in an ethics of care which embodies the notion of interdependent community.[36]

An ethics of care contrasts sharply with ethical theories in which the sense of self is separate from others and is reinforced by an individualistic ethics of rights emphasising autonomy and voluntary contractual relationships.[37] For cultural feminists, a contractual model of relationships, which is indifferent to fostering bonds of trust and caring, is an inappropriate means of governing relationships between strangers. An ethics of care provides a preferred framework for relationships, including that between doctor and patient. Within this moral framework, impartiality is not the hallmark of moral judgement and choice. According to a care perspective, moral problems cannot be solved solely by the application of abstract rules or principles. Instead, moral approaches should be tailored to particular situations.[38] Contextualized methods of reasoning are felt to assist understanding and exposure of injustices that might otherwise go unobserved. Katharine Bartlett suggests that "reasoning from context can change perceptions about the world, which may then

11

further expand the contexts within which such reasoning seems appropriate, which in turn may lead to still further changes in perceptions".[39] Whilst acknowledging that many decisions will be correctly arrived at by focusing on a particular context, Susan Sherwin cautions that when considering new reproductive technologies it will be necessary to define context in social and political terms. This will permit consideration of the effect of such medical interventions "on womens' pursuit of greater power in a society which currently subordinates them".[40]

There is disagreement as to whether rules or principles should be incorporated within an ethics of care. Caring, according to Nel Noddings, is not based on ethical principles or rules, but rather on the notion of an ideal self moulded with reference to one's own experience of caring and being cared for by others.[41] For others, an ethics of care devoid of rules or principles does not provide adequate safeguards against arbitrary and paternalistic behaviour.[42]

A suggested point of divergence between radical and cultural feminism relates to their differing interpretations of women's experience of connection with others. Radical feminists perceive women's connection with others as invasive and intrusive, giving rise to a desire for individuation.[43] According to Catherine MacKinnon:

> But she [Gilligan] achieves for moral reasoning what the special protection rule achieves in law: the affirmative rather than the negative valuation of that which has accurately distinguished women from men, by making it seem as though those attributes, with their consequences, really are somehow ours, rather than what male supremacy has attributed to us for its own use. For women to affirm difference, when difference means dominance, as it does with gender, means to affirm the qualities and characteristics of powerlessness...I do not think that the way women reason morally is morality "in a different voice". I think it is morality in a higher register, in the feminine voice. Women value care because men have valued us according to the care we give them... Women think in relational terms because our existence is defined in relation to men. Further, when you are powerless, you don't just speak differently....Your speech is not just differently articulated, it is silenced.[44]

Attempts to categorize feminist theory are not particularly meaningful for MacKinnon who argues that liberal feminism, rather than being a distinctive philosophy, has frequently been no more than liberalism applied to women. Similarly, socialist feminism has often amounted to no more than Marxism applied to women. Both ideologies have proved inadequate in the face of an all pervasive system of male dominance and control institutionalized by the State and reflected in legal norms.[45] The inadequacy of liberal feminism lies in its perception of sexism as an imbalance capable of adjustment by the securing of equal rights. Securing abstract rights for women is unsatisfactory because rights "authorize the male experience of the world".[46] She suggests that feminism should take the form of radical post-Marxist feminism, which aims "to uncover and claim as valid the experience of women, the male content of which is the devaluation of women's experience".[47] Others, including Robin West, perceive a need for a feminist jurisprudence premised on women's distinctive state of being which could conceivably incorporate a modified rights perspective.[48]

The exclusive focus on gender which characterizes much early feminist literature is rejected by some feminists on the grounds that it perpetuates the same kinds of biases which characterize male-normative theories.[49] Various alternatives have been suggested to avoid these theoretical shortcomings including a postmodern-feminist theory of identity in which gender is considered together with class, race, ethnicity, age, and sexual orientation.[50]

Although united in their criticism of medical paternalism, liberal, cultural and radical feminism differ in their views of common law regulation of the clinical relationship, including the role of patients as decision-makers. Each of these perspectives is discussed in particular contexts in subsequent chapters.

BIOETHICS

While the consumer and women's movements were gathering momentum, another force was developing which would significantly affect medical ethics. The emerging field of bioethics was clearly distinguishable from traditional medical ethics because of its interdisciplinary perspective and independence from professional control.[51] Not limited to an exchange of ideas in scholarly journals, bioethics includes wider professional and public concerns about ethical issues and has taken on some of the features of a social movement.[52]

Traditional medical ethics was largely contained in professional codes and oaths. There is disagreement about whether these codes may be properly regarded as embodying principles of etiquette rather than ethics, and rules rather than values.[53] Some argue, that prior to the emergence of bioethics, there had been no attempt to devise professional guidelines based on an established theory of ethics.[54] Consequently, the professional standards which evolved have been described as more akin to customs or mores, than to a system of ethics.[55]

Participants in bioethical discourse

Catholic, Protestant and Jewish moral theologians were the undoubted pioneers of medical ethics. In 1954, in a seminal work entitled **Morals and Medicine,** Joseph Fletcher, an Episcopalian theologian, commented that, except for the writings of Catholic moralists, a discussion of health and medical ethics was noticeably absent from almost all ethical literature.[56] Fletcher's work, with its focus on human rights, was subsequently described as "a disruptive Protestant challenge" to traditional Catholic medical ethics.[57] As might be expected, denominational differences were perpetuated in moral theories. Consequently, Catholic teachings and beliefs were not regarded as universally applicable.[58] In turn, Fletcher's work, particularly his rejection of the natural law, attracted Catholic criticism.[59]

During the following decade, Catholic and Protestant theologians did not publicly debate medical ethical issues. A possible explanation for their silence is a pre-occupation with the civil rights movement and, in the case of the Catholic theologians, the Second Vatican Council.[60]   Religious thinkers appear once again to have dominated medical ethics from 1965 until 1975, a period which has been termed "the renaissance of medical ethics".[61]   During this so-called renaissance, **The Patient as Person,** by Protestant ethicist Paul Ramsey, was published. This work focused on clinical and research relationships in medical practice. Intelligible to lay, academic, and theological audiences, it symbolized and popularized the renaissance of medical ethics in the United States.[62]

Some theological commentators attributed the depersonalization of the clinical relationship and the loss of concern for the moral aspects of practice to technological changes in medicine. Moreover, they contended that these changes raised important moral issues which should not be left solely to practitioners to determine. The opening up of medical ethics to outside scrutiny was a theme which would continue to occupy bioethicists and others during the following decades.

The secular nature of bioethics prompted Protestant theologian, James Gustafson, to suggest that theological contributions to medical ethics are likely to be of minimal importance. Gustafson argues that for most individuals involved in medical care and practice, moral principles and values can be justified without reference to God, whilst attitudes derived from religious beliefs can be developed in other ways.[63] For others, the predominantly secular nature of bioethical discourse threatens medicine as a moral practice. H. Tristram Engelhardt notes that even the contributions of Christian and Jewish religious thinkers to the bioethical debate contain "much reflection on bioethics which is not in the genre of Judeo-Christian religious thought in sensu stricto but which falls more in the genre of philosophy".[64]   Stanley Hauerwas suggests that, in analysing medical issues, theologians adopted philosophical terms, frequently minimizing their own moral views in the interests of communal harmony and consensus. This in turn reinforced the notion that theological perspectives are irrelevant to medicine.[65]

A problem for many individuals is that their beliefs will conflict with prevailing secular morality. Engelhardt argues that these individuals must live within two moral viewpoints as represented by their particular values and beliefs and by secular public morality. Although this will undoubtedly result in "moral schizophrenia", they are not entitled to choose one set of values in preference to the other, but must embrace both.[66]   Such a proposition is unacceptable to Hauerwas who believes that the nature of religious convictions will be transformed by their subordination to the prevailing ethos of freedom.[67]   Alternatively, a refusal to subordinate one's particular views and to insist they should guide medical practice will be at odds with the ethic of Engelhardt's 'peaceable community'.[68]   Faced with this dilemma, Hauerwas suggests that theologians have concerned themselves with procedural issues, and in so doing, have avoided the challenge of devising a morally worthy ethos for medical practice.[69]

For Hauerwas, medicine can only exist as a profession when it is supported by a community which has a commitment to care for the sick and dying.[70]   An ethics of care is an integral part of the practice of medicine and a doctor's willingness to be present in times of sickness cannot, he argues, be explained in Engelhardt's terms.[71] A continuing presence, as implied in an ethics of care, is a form of Christian ethics to assist others in times of hardship and suffering.[72]   Medicine, therefore, needs the church, "as a resource of the habits and practices necessary to sustain the care of those in pain".[73]

14

Recently, there appears to be a renewed interest in examining the contribution of theology to bioethics.[74] For some, the relevance of a theological perspective in bioethics lies in the contribution that a specific Christian virtue such as charity can bring to moral choices in a medical context.[75] For others, theological perspectives play an important role in pluralist societies by acting as a counter-balance to the adoption of minimalist moral standards.[76] A small number of philosophers and moral theologians developed ethical framework incorporating an ethics of virtue. For these individuals, ethics should not primarily focus on notions of obligation, rules and judgements of right and wrong, but rather on the importance of having an appropriate motive and desire for morally correct action. Some of these individuals argue that whilst duty-based and virtue ethics have different emphases, they can, and should, provide mutually re-enforcing ethical frameworks.[77]

The newly emerging bioethics provided philosophers with an opportunity to become involved in problems of normative ethics.[78] From the mid-seventies onwards, the work of analytical philosophers overshadowed those whose work reflected a more social or theological perspective. A possible explanation for this is that their rational and objective approach complemented that of lawyers who were also becoming involved in bioethical issues at this time. Stephen Toulmin suggests that this theoretical phase continued until the late eighties and that thereafter bioethics became more practical in its orientation.[79] In the following section, selected views from bioethical literature and debate are outlined.

Bioethical theories and perspectives

Autonomy and "the peaceable community"

Various attempts have been made to devise theoretical frameworks for pluralist societies lacking a rational consensus on ethical issues. In 'the peaceable community', a theoretical model developed by H. Tristram Engelhardt, individuals are free to make moral choices, regardless of how unwise they may appear to others. Infliction of harm and the forceful imposition of a particular moral view on others are contrary to the notion of the 'peaceable community'.[80]

Although it is impossible to devise a commonly accepted set of values, Engelhardt believes that it is possible to establish an authoritative consensus regarding acceptable conduct.[81] This may be achieved by reliance on procedural rather than substantive issues. Consistent with the prevailing ethos of freedom, the role of ethics should be limited to analysis and clarification as opposed to determining substantive matters of moral content or normative prescriptions.[82] Consequently, in the "peaceable community", secular morality is concerned with procedures protecting free choice rather than with the morality of the choice itself. This means that certain "natural rights" including contraception, abortion and suicide are regarded as matters of private as opposed to public morality.[83]

When individuals interact as moral strangers, there is little likelihood that trust will develop, so moral constraints are necessary. As Alasdair McIntyre suggests :

Where a community of moral and metaphysical beliefs is lacking, trust between strangers becomes much more questionable than when we can safely assume such a community. Nobody can rely on anyone else's judgements on his or her behalf until he or she knows what the other person believes. It follows that nobody can accept the moral authority of another in virtue simply of his professional position. We are thrust back by our social conditions into a form of moral autonomy.[84]

In these circumstances, Engelhardt argues that rules are necessary to guard against misunderstandings and abuses of power.[85] James Childress contends that a community of moral strangers does not necessarily preclude trust. Common agreement about rules and procedural safeguards will permit practitioners and patients to come together as friendly strangers.[86] Patient trust, he believes, may then be expressed as a faith in practitioners to adhere to guidelines based on principles of justice and respect for others.[87]

A paternalistic model of medicine is incompatible with the ethos of freedom in the "peaceable community". For Englehardt, the role of medical practitioners is akin to that of mediators who offer advice on the consequences of possible choices, without substituting their own moral preferences for those of the patient. Although authority in the "peaceable community" is a matter of contractual agreement, establishing covenantal bonds to the mutual satisfaction of both parties may not be possible when parties do not share common values. One suggestion for overcoming this problem is for practitioners to become affiliated with institutions sharing similar values. An advance declaration of institutional values would redress some of the problems arising out of relationships between moral strangers as patients could approach practitioners and institutions with a clearer understanding of the moral values guiding practice.[88]

Plotting the limits of autonomy - autonomy v community

The emphasis on autonomy and rights found in bioethical literature and debate is also evident in the social attitudes and political philosophy of the sixties. As Daniel Callahan, Director of the Hastings Bioethics Center, New York observes:

The antipaternalism that is at least one of the natural children of autonomy is hardly unique to the medical sphere; it is at one with the skepticism toward authority, especially moral authority, that has marked the past two decades.[89]

For Callahan and others, an emphasis on autonomy has been at the expense of the development of moral obligations for individuals as community members. Overvaluing autonomy has created "a minimalist ethic" according to which individuals are subject to few constraints. In the resulting moral climate, obligations are confined to those of family and those which are freely assumed. Moreover, in a community of moral strangers, there is no room for extra-contractual commitments such as altruism, beneficence or self-sacrifice.[90] Callahan contends that emphasis on autonomy, together with the recognition of contractual relations as the principal form of obligations between individuals, inevitably diminishes the sense of community.[91]

Virtue-based ethics - beneficence in trust

An ethical model balancing patient autonomy and practitioner beneficence employing the concept of beneficence in trust has been devised by Edmund Pellegrino and David Thomasma.[92] Whilst welcoming increased patient participation in decision-making, they nevertheless caution against the presumption that where medical beneficence and patient autonomy conflict, autonomy must always prevail.[93] Believing that the moral basis of medicine is threatened by enhancing individualism at the expense of other values, they prefer a beneficence-based model as a means of allocating rights and responsibilities between doctors and their patients.[94]

Paternalism is rejected as a generally unsuitable model for medical decision-making because it overrides respect for individuals, and assumes that medical good is absolute. However, in certain treatment decisions involving elderly, senile patients and children a paternalistic approach may be appropriate. They argue that an autonomy model of decision-making is not appropriate in emergency situations and in the case of incompetent patients. Furthermore, it fails to take account of the extent to which illness may affect self-determination. Determining the psycho-social impact of disease on a patient's personal and moral status, is necessary both to avoid acts of paternalism and to ensure that patients are not "abandoned to their autonomy".[95]

The beneficence in trust model endorses a best interests approach which respects patient autonomy, and incorporates a benefits to burdens calculation concerning a patient's quality of life.[96] Priority is given to a patient's needs in all but the most exceptional circumstances. This means that choice as to whether to foster autonomy or to act paternalistically is governed by what will most benefit a patient, rather than by a practitioner's intellectual convictions or moral values.[97] According to this approach, clinical practice incorporates both patient autonomy and beneficial paternalism. The former may be appropriately exercised when diagnosis and options are clear. Beneficial paternalism is required when diagnosis, prognosis, or treatment are uncertain. In these circumstances, it may be necessary for doctors to make recommendations based on intuitive assessments. However, by acknowledging the uncertainties which confront them, it is argued that doctors' actions are beneficent, not paternalistic.[98]

Limitations of the autonomy-model of decision-making

The secular and pluralist nature of society accounts for the widespread appeal of the autonomy model of decision-making. In the absence of consensus on substantive issues, there has been an emphasis on procedures to avoid the possibility of doctors and other authority figures overriding patients' wishes. The authors believe that it is futile to separate analytical from normative ethics as analytical ethics cannot escape

17

from the normative assertion that autonomy is the overriding principle. Despite certain pragmatic attractions, procedure cannot be self-justifying so that it will always be necessary to determine whether what is procedurally correct, is also morally justifiable.[99]

The value placed on autonomy in Engelhardt's 'peaceable society' engenders private morality. Like Callahan, Pellegrino and Thomasma believe that the resulting 'moral atomism' threatens the sense of community, so that a quest for the common good is abandoned. They caution that by acknowledging the importance of freedom of choice, a society does not escape the need to develop some common moral goals in addition to autonomy.[100] This is because the importance of autonomy is not derived from an exercise of self-determination by isolated individuals, but rather from choices made by individuals who are community members. In their view, although choice creates an individually interpreted morality, moral choices and values originate from, and return to, the community.[101]

Beneficence in medical decisions

An underlying principle of the beneficence model is that doctors must act according to competent patients' wishes, unless such a course of action would be morally repugnant. This obligation is further qualified by social constraints and public policy concerning health care.[102] The fundamental aim of medicine is to provide "a right and good healing action" for each patient, which is consistent with individuals united in community.[103] In addition to conforming with canons of good medicine, treatment includes paying attention to the psychological, social and spiritual dimensions of the disease or injury. Health is a relational, rather than an absolute, good arising out of the commitments doctor and patient make to each other so that a patient's own values may override this good.[104] It is also a negotiable good which necessitates an on-going dialogue. In the event that agreement is not possible, parties are free to withdraw.[105]

Beneficence in trust

Beneficence in trust expands the notion of beneficence to include additional ethical principles. Because beneficence includes respecting patients' wishes, it is distinguishable from, and cannot lead to, paternalism. As the fundamental principle guiding care, beneficence may be overridden by extra-medical values only in exceptional circumstances.[106] Beneficence in trust is based on an ethics of virtue, in preference to an ethics of rules. For Pellegrino and Thomasma, the mere existence of rules does not guarantee their observance. Because an ethics of virtue, without more, may reduce ethics to the habits or dispositions of individuals, they acknowledge a need for guidelines based on communities of practice.[107] Whilst recognizing that medicine practised in conformity with virtue-based ethics may result in unwelcome intrusions, indistinguishable from self-righteous paternalism, they argue that virtuous practitioners can be expected to be more sensitive to such possibilities than others whose ethics are deontologically or legally oriented.[108]

Linking virtue-based with rights and duty-based ethics

The moral effectiveness of rights and duties ultimately depends upon the character of those carrying out the duties. In order to adequately protect patients' good, Pellegrino and Thomasma contend that virtue-based ethics must be linked with rights and duty-based ethics. The relationships between these ethical models should be clearly stated in professional codes. Explicitness should encourage greater honesty between doctors and their patients as specific statements would reduce the opportunity for practitioners to pay mere lip service to general code provisions. Patient choice would be assisted, as patients would be able to seek out doctors on the basis of their ethical commitments, as well as their expertise.[109]

The interdependence of virtue-based and rights and duty-based ethics is succinctly explained as follows:

> The more we yearn for ethical sensitivity, the less we lean on rights, duties, rules, and principles and the more on the character traits of the moral agent. Paradoxically, without rules, rights, and duties specifically spelled out, we cannot predict what form a particular person's expression of virtue will take. In a pluralistic society, ... principles and professional standards ought to assure a dependable minimum level of moral conduct. But that minimum level is insufficient in the complex, often unpredictable circumstances of decision-making, where technical and value desiderata intersect so inextricably.[110]

The model devised by Pellegrino and Thomasma stresses trust and seeks to encourage a relationship more akin to a joint enterprise or mutual endeavour. Such a model presupposes that intimate, ongoing relationships are possible. The nature of health care delivery, especially in the case of team care of public hospital patients, makes this kind of relationship difficult, if not impossible, to achieve.

The authors recognize that medical decisions by patients are subject to external constraints. Clearly difficulties will be encountered by patients and their doctors when they believe that social limits, sanctioned by law, are unreasonable. The problem of how tensions of this nature may be resolved is not satisfactorily addressed by this model.

Bioethics - boon or bane?

A note of caution has been sounded by the Reverend Professor Gordon Dunstan, who regards the new medical ethics as lacking a base in practical experience, and as having usurped a moral authority properly belonging to the medical profession.[111] For others, the purpose of bioethics is not to usurp the moral authority of the medical profession by providing a system of incontrovertible principles. Instead, bioethical principles are regarded more akin to guidelines or persuasive precedents. Rather than posing a threat to medicine, bioethics can assist in the selection, interpretation, and application of appropriate ethical principles to particular issues.[112] According to this view, bioethics and medicine can develop a symbiotic relationship in which shared skills contribute to the construction of an ethical framework for medical practice.[113]

OVERVIEW

Public attitudes towards the medical profession both in Australia and the United States have changed significantly during the last three decades. Doctors are no longer presumed to be in the best position to make decisions on behalf of patients. Rather, it is now widely believed that patients themselves must assume responsibility for decisions which affect their bodies.

Rejection of medical paternalism began with challenges to the professional monopoly over medical decision-making by moral theologians, consumer and women's groups. During the seventies, American consumer groups argued for participatory decision-making and were instrumental in the FDA's decision to include lay representatives on prescription drug advisory committees. This, together with the inclusion of non-medical representatives on American and Australian research ethics committees, signalled a recognition by regulatory authorities in both countries that scientific decision-making should no longer be the exclusive concern of medical experts.

As the notion of rights took hold in American society in the wake of the civil rights movement, consumer organizations drafted Bills of Health Rights. Similar documents were drafted by Australian consumer organizations. Emphasis was placed on the provision of information in these documents in an effort to ensure that patients were involved in clinical decision-making.

Some of the articulated rights were in the nature of legal entitlements enforceable at common law. Consumer groups and liberal feminists endorsed a rights model as a suitable framework for the doctor-patient relationship. This model was rejected by radical feminists and others, as an inadequate endorsement of patient self-determination. In order to compensate for the perceived inadequacies of a rights model of decision-making, they sought to develop theoretical perspectives incorporating the notion of patients as autonomous agents.

Certain philosophers and moral theologians view the doctor-patient relationship as a mutual undertaking in which the parties make a commitment to work towards the common goal of the patient's health. An insistence on autonomy is regarded as detrimental to this relationship as it overlooks medical beneficence and may encourage the abandonment of patients in time of need.[114]

An ethics of rights also contrasts with an ethics of care which contextualizes methods of reasoning and emphasises relationships and responsibilities between individuals. Despite differences between these perspectives, various attempts have been made to incorporate rules within virtue and care-based ethical frameworks.

The importance of these widely-differing perspectives is that they have created a framework for public debate. This, in turn, has influenced, albeit in differing degrees, the development of common law precedents, statutory standards and non-legislative guidelines pertaining to decision-making in clinical and research contexts. These developments are traced in the following chapters. In Chapter Two, the development of American and Australian common law in the area of information disclosure is outlined. The chapter also explores the extent to which autonomy and rights-based concepts have been incorporated into the law in both countries. Common law standards are compared with Australian non-legislative guidelines which contain a broad range of ideas and theoretical perspectives. The influence of rights and autonomy-based arguments and an ethics of care perspective on Victorian legislative standards governing treatment refusal is explored in Chapter Three. This chapter also documents the influence of these views on American common law and statutory standards. Regulation of human subject research in Australia and America is discussed in Chapter Four. The recent challenge to traditional ethical assumptions underlying human subject research and regulation precipitated by the AIDS crisis is the subject-matter of Chapter Five.

Notes

1. Starr P, The Social Transformation of American Medicine. Basic Books Inc. 1982, 389.
2. Id.393.
3. Ibid.
4. Kirby Mr. Justice M., Changes in Professionalism. Australian Medical Association Gazette, May 1, 1980, 20-1. Report of the Task Force to Review the Structure, Function and Constitution of the Australian Medical Association. February, 1987, Chapter 5.
5. Haug M. and Lavin B., Consumerism in Medicine: Challenging Physician Authority. Sage Publications 1983,10.
6. Darvall L., Consumer Participation in Government Decision-making: New Drug Evaluation in Australia and the United States. 6 Journal of Consumer Policy 1986, 41 - 55.
7. The regulations are discussed in Chapter Four.
8. Rothman D., Strangers at the Bedside: A History of How Law and Bioethics Transformed Medical Decision-Making. Basic Books Inc. 1991, 211-21.
9. Betz M. and O'Connell L., Changing Doctor-Patient Relationships and the Rise in Concern for Accountability. 31 Social Problems 1983, 84.
10. Faden R. and Beauchamp T., A History and Theory of Informed Consent. Oxford University Press 1986,93.
11. Hamilton P., Health Care Consumerism. The C.V. Mosby Company. Toronto 1982, 81-3.
12. The Australian Consumers Association and the Australian Federation of Consumer Organizations are concerned with health issues at national and international levels. The Consumers' Health Forum was established by the

Federal government in response to a demand for public participation in health policy formulation. The Victorian Health Issues Centre, an independent non-government policy analysis and advocacy organization, is also concerned with consumer rights issues, complaints and women's health policy.

13.   A.C.T. Charter of Patient Rights and Responsibilities. Appendix 1.

14.   Legal Recognition and Protection of the Rights of Health Consumers. Consumers' Health Forum of Australia Inc. 1990.

15.   Faden and Beauchamp, op.cit. 94.

16.   Ibid.

17.   Dunstan G.R., Evolution and Mutation in Medical Ethics, in Ethical Dilemmas in Health Promotion. Doxiadis S.(ed.), John Wiley and Sons 1987,4.

18.   Green G., Patient's rights: power and dependency. 11 The Australian Nurses Journal 1982, 43-4.

19.   Rothman, op.cit. 147.

20.   Gordon L., What's New in Women's History, in Feminist Studies/ Critical Studies. T de Lauretis (ed.), 1986, 20, 38, as cited in Bartlett K., Feminist Legal Methods 103 Harvard Law Review 1990, 829, 833.

21.   Albury R., Reproductive Technology and Feminism. 89 Australian Left Review 1984, 46, 48.

22.   Fisher S., In the Patient's Best Interest: Women and the Politics of Medical Decisions. Rutgers University Press. New Jersey 1986,150.

23.   Fee E., Women and Health: The Politics of Sex in Medicine. Farmingdale: Baywood Publishing Company,1983, as cited in Fisher, op.cit. 151.

24.   Why Women's Health? Report of the Victorian Women's Health Working Party.1987,47.

25.   Other types of feminism include marxist feminism, spiritual feminism which concerns women's alternative consciousness, ecofeminism and pacifist feminism which link women's distaste for aggression with concerns for nature and nurture and conservative feminism which seeks to re-establish women's domestic role. Held V., Feminism and Moral Theory, in Kittay E. and Myers D. (eds), Women and Moral Theory. Rowman and Littlefield 1987,263.

26.   Because the majority of these cases are not reported, it is difficult to obtain an accurate estimate. Up until mid-1987, thirteen such court orders had been granted. The medical reasons given included foetal distress, previous caesarean section and placenta previa. Developments in the Law - Medical Technology and the Law 103 Harvard Law Review 1990,1567.

27.   Re A.C. 533 A.2d.611 (1987). The court subsequently granted a petition for rehearing, In the Matter of A.C. 539 A 2d.203 (1988)

28.   Brahams D., A Baby's Life or a Mother's Liberty: A United States Case. The Lancet, April 30, 1988,1006; McLean S., Women, Rights and Reproduction, in Legal Issues in Human Reproduction. McLean S.(ed.), Gower Press 1989, 213.

29.   Gallagher J., Prenatal Invasions and Interventions: What's Wrong With Fetal Rights 10 Harvard Woman's Law Journal 1987, 58.

30.   Rhoden, The Judge in the Delivery Room: The Emergence of Court-Ordered Caesareans. 74 California Law Review 1986, 1951, as cited in Developments in the Law, op.cit. 1572.

31.   In Re A.C. 573 A 2d. 1235, 1990

32. Id.at 1252. Substituted judgement is discussed in Chapter Three.
33. West R., Jurisprudence and Gender. 55 University of Chicago Law Review 1988 1,14.
34. Id.16-7. see also Alcoff L., Cultural Feminism Versus Post-Structuralism: The Identity Crisis in Feminist Theory. 13 Signs: Journal of Women in Culture and Society 1988, 405.
35. Gilligan C., In A Different Voice. Harvard University Press 1982,74, 159-60.
36. Gilligan, op.cit. 19,156; West, op.cit. 28.
37. Gilligan op.cit. 21. Gilligan suggests that recent studies indicate that the justice and care perspectives described in In a Different Voice do not correlate strictly with gender. Gilligan C., Ward J. and Taylor J.(eds) Mapping the Moral Domain. Harvard University Press. 1988. Although some commentators refer to "an ethic of care", the term "an ethics of care" is used throughout this narrative.
38. Held, op.cit. 120; Wolf S., Nancy Beth Cruzan: In no voice at all. 20 Hastings Center Report 1990, 38.
39. Bartlett, op.cit. 863.
40. Sherwin S., Feminist and Medical Ethics: Two Different Approaches to Contextual Ethics, in Feminist Perspectives in Medical Ethics. Holmes H.B. and Purdy L. (eds). Indiana University Press 1992, 17, 27; Rowland R., Choice, Control and Issues of Informed Consent: The New Reproductive and Pre-Birth Technologies.Informed Consent Symposia, Law Reform Commission of Victoria 1988, 102.
41. Noddings N., Caring - A Feminine Approach to Ethics and Moral Education. University of California Press 1984, 94. Susan Sherwin comments that whilst Noddings is not a feminist, her contribution to the theoretical development of an ethics of care is acknowledged by feminists scholars, Sherwin, op.cit. 19, n.3.
42. For an interesting analysis of an ethics of care and its relationship to an ethics of rights see Carse A., The 'Voice of Care': Implications For Bioethical Education 16 The Journal of Medicine and Philosophy 1991, 5.
43. West, op. cit. 15, 38.
44. MacKinnon C., Feminism Unmodified. Harvard University Press 1987, 38-9 as cited in Graycar R. and Morgan J.(eds), The Hidden Gender of Law. The Federation Press 1990, 53.
45. MacKinnon C. Feminism, Marxism, Method, and the State : Toward Feminist Jurisprudence. 8 Signs - Journal of Women in Culture and Society, 1983. 635, 639-40.
46. Id.640-2, 658.
47. Id.638.
48. West, op. cit. 61, 41.
49. Bordo S., Feminism, Postmodernism, and Gender-Scepticism, in Feminism/ Postmodernism. Nicholson L.(ed.), Routledge 1990,138.
50. Id.139. Bordo cautions against such an approach commenting that as most institutions have barely begun to come to grips with modernist social criticism, it is too soon to absolve them from further responsibility via "postmodern heterogeneity and instability" Id.153.

51. Faden and Beauchamp, op.cit. 92. For a useful comparative discussion of the development of bioethics in the United States and Britain see Biomedical Ethics: An Anglo American Dialogue. 530 Annals of the New York Academy of Sciences 1988.

52. Fox R., The Evolution of American Bioethics: A Sociological Perspective, in Weisz G. (ed.), Social Science Perspectives on Medical Ethics. Kluwer Academic Publishers 1990, 201.

53. Flather-Morgan A., The Renaissance of Medical Ethics: The Emergence of the Bioethics Movement in the Late 1960s. M.D. Thesis, Yale University School of Medicine 1989, 1,6,18. This section is heavily indebted to the historical material and insightful analysis contained in this thesis; Jonsen A. and Hellegers A., Conceptual Foundations for an Ethic of Medical Care, in Veatch R. and Branson R. (eds), Ethics and Health Policy. Ballinger Publishing Company 1976, 19-22.

54. Flather-Morgan, op.cit. 13.

55. Id.22. Other critics suggest that traditional medical ethics did not take into account the theory of the common good. Id.21. The danger of evaluating moral concepts apart from their historical context is elaborated upon at Id.18-21.

56. Fletcher J., Morals and Medicine. Princeton University Press 1954,16, as cited in Flather-Morgan, op.cit. 26.

57. Walters L., Religion and the Renaissance of Medical Ethics in the United States: 1965-1975, in Theology and Bioethics. Shelp E.D.(ed.), 3-16, Reidel Publishing Company Boston 1985, as cited in Flather-Morgan, op.cit. 37.

58. Flather-Morgan, op.cit. 27.

59. Id.38.

60. Walters, op.cit. 6, as cited in Flather-Morgan, op.cit. 39.

61. Walters, op.cit. 3, as cited in Flather-Morgan op.cit. 37.

62. Walters, op.cit. 12, as cited in Flather-Morgan op.cit. 47.

63. Gustafson J.M., The Contributions of Theology to Medical Ethics. Marquette University Press 1975 93-4, as cited in Campbell C.S., Theological integrity and philosophical pluralism in medical ethics. 2 Medical Humanities Review 1988, 49.

64. Engelhardt H.T., Bioethics in Pluralist Societies. 26 Perspectives in Biology and Medicine 1983, 64.

65. Hauerwas S., The Suffering Presence. University of Notre Dame Press 1986, 74.

66. Engelhardt, op.cit. 76-7.

67. Hauerwas, op.cit. 11.

68. The notion of the "peaceable community" is described in the following section.

69. Hauerwas, op.cit. 74.

70. Id.52.

71. Id.13.

72. Id.80.

73. Id.81.

74. McCormick R.A., Theology and Bioethics. 19 Hastings Center Report 1989, 5. A conference which explored the relevance of theological perspectives for bioethics was held at the Hastings Center, New York in May, 1989.

75. Pellegrino E., Agape and Ethics: Some Reflections on Medical Morals from a Catholic Christian (forthcoming) in Catholic Perspectives on Medical Morals: Foundational Issues v.34 Kluwer Academic Publishers, as cited in McCormick, op.cit. 8 n.18.

76. Lammers S.E. and Verhey A.E. Grand Rapids Michigan 1987, as cited in Campbell C.S., op. cit.49, 50.

77. Beauchamp T.L., and Childress J.F. Principles of Biomedical Ethics. Oxford University Press 1989, 374-85; Pellegrino E., Character, Virtue and Self-Interest in the Ethics of the Professions. 5 The Journal of Contemporary Health Law and Policy 1989, 53, 72.

78. Toulmin S., How Medicine Saved the Life of Ethics. 25 Perspectives in Biology and Medicine 1982, 736.

79. Toulmin S., Medical Ethics in its American Context-An Historical Survey. 530 Annals of the New York Academy of Sciences 1988, 7, 13-5.

80. Engelhardt, op.cit. 65, 66-70.

81. Engelhardt H.T., The Foundations of Bioethics. Oxford University Press. 1986, 251. (Hereinafter cited as The Foundations of Bioethics)

82. Engelhardt, The Foundations of Bioethics. op.cit., as cited in Pellegrino E. and Thomasma D., For The Patient's Good-The Restoration of Beneficence in Health Care. Oxford University Press 1988, 21. (Hereinafter cited as For The Patient's Good)

83. Engelhardt, The Foundation of Bioethics, op.cit. 47-8.

84. McIntyre A., Patients as Agents, in Philosophical Medical Ethics, Its Nature and Significance: Proceedings of the Third Trans-Disciplinary Symposium on Philosophy and Medicine. Spicker S. and Engelhardt H.T.(eds), D.Reidel Publishing Co. 1977, 197, 210.

85. Engelhardt, The Foundations of Bioethics, op.cit. 260-1.

86. Childress J., Who Should Decide ? Paternalism in Health Care. Oxford University Press 1982,49; Childress J., The Normative Principles of Medical Ethics in Veatch R.(ed.), Medical Ethics. Jones and Bartlett 1989, 29, 43.

87. Childress, Who Should Decide ?, op.cit. 48.

88. Mc Intyre, op.cit. 197. see also Veatch R., Contemporary Bioethics and the Demise of Modern Medicine. Bioethics News 1989, 18-9.

89. Callahan D., Autonomy: A Moral Good, Not A Moral Obsession. 14 Hastings Center Report 1984, 40,42.

90. Callahan D., Minimalist Ethics, 11 Hastings Center Report 1981, 19,20.

91. Callahan, Autonomy :A Moral Good, Not A Moral Obsession, op.cit. 41.

92. Pellegrino and Thomasma, For The Patient's Good, op.cit. 4-5.

93. Id.5-6.

94. Id.49, 20.

95. Id.17.

96. Id.20. The 'best interests' test is discussed in Chapter Three in the context of treatment refusal.

97. Id.32.

98. Id.14.

99. Id.21-22.

100. Id.21-22.

101. Id.42.
102. Id.76.
103. Id.10, 42-3.
104. Id.40.
105. Id.33-4.
106. Id.55.
107. Id.53.
108. Id.122.
109. Id.124.
110. Id.122.
111. Dunstan G.R., Evolution and Mutation in Medical Ethics, in Ethical Dilemmas in Health Promotion. Doxiadis S.(ed.), John Wiley and Sons 1987, 12.
112. Charlesworth M., Morals and Medicine. 6 Bioethics News 1987 9; Toulmin S., The Tyranny of Principles. 11 Hastings Center Report 1981, 31.
113. Charlesworth, op.cit. 9.
114. Bergsma J. and Thomasma D., Health Care: Its Psychosocial Dimensions. Duquesne University Press 1982, as cited in Pellegrino and Thomasma, op.cit. 6; Hauerwas, op.cit. 81.

2 Consent to Medical Treatment

INTRODUCTION

The doctrine of informed consent emerged from American common law in the mid-fifties. Embodying the notion that a legally effective authorization for treatment must be voluntary, and arise from a patient's understanding of the risks of and alternatives to treatment, it imposes a legal duty on doctors to communicate information to their patients about risks and treatment options. In the hands of the American judiciary, it signalled the recognition of a legal right to information as part of the principle of self-determination. The concept rapidly became a focal point in legal, medical, bioethical, consumer and feminist literature and debate where, in the course of efforts to free it from its legal confines, it was subject to varying interpretations.

From the sixties onwards, changes in societal attitudes towards all forms of authority were reflected in debates concerning medical autonomy and accountability. A fundamental issue was the relative weight to be accorded to practitioner and patient autonomy in the clinical relationship. An emerging consensus suggested that a traditional, paternalistic model of medical care, was no longer appropriate for the clinical relationship, not the least because it was premised on practitioner beneficence, and accorded little weight to patient self-determination.

The notion of patients as autonomous agents transformed them from passive recipients of information to active and equal participants in treatment decisions. Consumers, bioethicists and others challenged the notion that medical decision-making involved an exclusive exercise of clinical judgement and expertise. Although essential for diagnosis, prognosis and treatment, medical expertise was not regarded as necessary for treatment comparisons, or for making a final treatment choice. Decisions about these matters were felt to be more appropriately based on a patient's particular values, beliefs and preferences. In short, the concept of patient self-

27

determination demanded that individual values and beliefs, no matter how seemingly irrational to others, should ultimately determine patient choice.

Informed decision-making is premised on the provision of adequate information. Various Australian inquiries conducted during the eighties, indicated patient dissatisfaction with the amount of information received, as well as communication problems between doctors and patients.[1] In contrast, practitioner submissions to a joint Law Reform Commission reference on Informed Consent suggested a general level of patient satisfaction with the information disclosure. The Commissions noted however, that while most doctors acknowledged the importance of providing information to patients, considerable variations in disclosure practices were evident.[2]

Information disclosure in the clinical relationship became of sufficient public interest and significance during the eighties for disclosure legislation relating to specific categories of patients to be enacted in three Australian States.[3] It was also the subject matter of a joint Law Reform Commissions' reference. Interestingly, the Commissions' first discussion paper was entitled **Informed Consent to Medical Treatment.** The reference to an American legal concept in the title is particularly striking because the doctrine of informed consent has not been incorporated into the Australian common law. A further link with American legal doctrine is contained within the document, as evidenced by the following comment:

> Our society recognizes the general moral notion that all people are autonomous beings who have a right to, and indeed should, make their own decisions. In the field of medical treatment this means that a competent adult person is entitled to decide what shall be done with his or her own body. ....A doctor should therefore give a patient sufficient information for the patient to understand the nature of any proposed treatment, its implications and risks, and the consequences of not taking the treatment. In the light of that information, it is the patient who should decide what treatment, if any, he or she will undertake. This is called an informed consent.[4]

This paragraph bears a close resemblance to a much-quoted statement of Justice Cardozo in 1914 in Schloendorff v Society of New York Hospital, an early American medical case.[5] As such, it signals a departure from the notion that the profession ought to be the sole arbiter for determining what is in the best interests of patients, and a clear recognition of patient autonomy and a right of self-determination.

At the close of the eighties, in addition to State statutory provisions, there was a handful of Australian common law decisions concerning information disclosure which reveal a cautious approach to the presumptions and concepts referred to in the Commissions' first paper. Why this is so is not entirely clear. It is true that Australian courts have had little opportunity to develop new standards of information disclosure because of the small number of cases coming before them. In addition, they are confined by a framework of negligence law. This explanation does not provide an entirely satisfactory answer, since the doctrine of informed consent, incorporating a rhetoric of self-determination and patient's rights, evolved from the American courts despite similar common law constraints. A more probable explanation is that the absence of Australian judicial activism in this regard is due both to the lack of a

Constitutional Bill of Rights, and a developed rights jurisprudence, such as that which has evolved in America. In the following sections, the development of Australian and American common law is briefly outlined.

AUSTRALIAN COMMON LAW REGULATION OF INFORMATION DISCLOSURE

The tort of battery

An action in battery is concerned with protecting individuals from unauthorized interferences. The notion of consent is so defined that if a patient consents in broad terms to medical treatment, failure to provide information of an inherent risk will not usually be regarded as denying the validity of the consent.[6] An interference need not have resulted in injury to be actionable. An offensive touching, in the absence of injury, may amount to battery. Although it must be established that the defendant was responsible for the interference complained of, causation is not required to be established in the same manner as in a negligence action, where it creates substantial difficulties for plaintiffs in terms of proof. Negligence now appears to be the preferred cause of action in cases concerning information disclosure.[7] The demise of battery claims against medical practitioners probably stems from the fact that these actions are frequently concerned with deliberately hostile interferences with others which run counter to the medical obligation of care.

The tort of negligence

The tort of negligence provides redress for injuries suffered as the result of negligent statements, acts or omissions. Negligence law is defined in terms of a responsibility or duty of care not to injure another, rather than in terms of a right not to be injured. Whilst every legal duty has a correlative right, courts in Australia and in the United Kingdom proceed from a duty rather than a rights perspective. Nevertheless, the duty to disclose information is premised on a patient's moral right to choose whether to accept or refuse treatment.[8] A duty perspective is more consistent with a paternalistic model of medical decision-making than is the rights orientation of the American courts which underscores patient self-determination.

In a negligence action, courts balance professional expertise and judgement against the competing concept of patient self-determination. This process has been recognized by one Australian Judge, Chief Justice King, who suggests that in determining the extent of the duty to disclose, "the duty of the doctor to act in what he conceives to be the best interests of the patient," is to be considered together with "the right of the patient to control his own life and to have the information necessary to do so".[9]

Judicial acknowledgement of a patient's right to information are rare both in Australia and the United Kingdom. Chief Justice King has stated that the paramount consideration in determining the scope of the duty to disclose "is the right of every human being to make the decisions which affect his own life and welfare and to determine the risks which he is willing to undertake".[10] In Sidaway v Governors of Bethlem Royal Hospital, Lord Scarman recognized such a right in the following terms:

> The doctor's duty arises from his patient's rights. If one considers the scope of the doctor's duty by beginning with the right of the patient to make his own decision whether he will or will not undergo the treatment proposed, the right to be informed of significant risk and the doctor's corresponding duty are easy to understand. [11]

The reasonable doctor test of disclosure

In defining a duty to disclose, Australian courts have adopted a dual standard whereby the amount and type of information given must accord with what a reasonable doctor would give to a reasonable patient in the circumstances of the particular patient. The measuring of conduct against the standard of a reasonable person is an objective test. The reasonable doctor standard requires that a doctor must explain what he intends to do and the implications of the treatment, in the way a careful and responsible doctor in similar circumstances would do.[12] Information and advice provided must conform with current medical practice and must include material risks.[13] These are defined as "matters which might influence the decisions of a reasonable person in the situation of the patient".[14] Included are "real risks of misfortune inherent in the treatment" together with any real risk that the treatment might be ineffective.[15]

When disclosing information, doctors should take into account a patient's state of health, personality, temperament, level of understanding, and expressed or apparent desire for information.[16] Gender, ethnicity, values, beliefs and preferences are noticeably absent.[17] Although not expressly referred to in the relevant cases, an argument for their inclusion could be made on the basis of Chief Justice King's statement that the category of listed factors is not exhaustive.[18] Moreover, the requirement that a doctor disclose matters which might affect a reasonable person in the situation of the particular patient could arguably include values, preferences and beliefs.

The importance of beliefs and values in forming part of a patient's decision, was specifically referred to by Lord Scarman in Sidaway's case as follows:

> It is ... a sound and reasonable proposition that the doctor should be required to exercise care in respecting the patient's right of decision. He must acknowledge that in very many cases factors other than the purely medical will play a significant part in his patient's decision-making process ....a patient may well have in mind circumstances, objectives, and values which he may reasonably not make known to the doctor but which may

lead him to a different decision from that suggested by purely medical opinion.[19]

The role of expert evidence in establishing professional standards

In Australia, a legal standard of reasonable care governs acts and omissions, as well as advice. The standard which the courts apply is that of an "ordinarily careful and competent practitioner of the class to which the practitioner belongs".[20] Courts in the United Kingdom, relying on the so-called Bolam test, place greater weight on standard medical practice as evidence of reasonable conduct. This test provides that if a doctor acts in accordance with a practice accepted as reasonable by a responsible body of medical opinion, he or she will not have acted in a negligent manner.[21]

In the Sidaway case, a majority of the House of Lords approved the Bolam test. In that case, the plaintiff became severely disabled by partial paralysis following a spinal operation. She argued that had she been warned of the risks of damage to the spinal cord and to a nerve root, which posed a danger of pain and weakness in the legs, she would not have consented to the operation. The risk of either type of damage occurring was estimated at between one and two per cent. Although she was able to provide medical evidence which suggested that the surgeon ought to have warned of leg weakness and continuing arm pain, other expert evidence suggested that non-disclosure of the risk to the spinal cord was supported by a responsible body of medical opinion. As a result, Mrs Sidaway failed to establish her case. Although the Bolam test was relied on by the court, three of the judges suggested that, in the case of substantial risks, it would be open to a court to conclude, despite any reasonable body of medical opinion to the contrary, that a patient should have been informed.

Recent Australian decisions indicate that evidence of a general or approved medical practice will not necessarily be conclusive in law as to whether it is negligent.[22] This is because the courts are aware that professional disclosure practices may evolve with an eye to protecting the interests of the profession rather than the interests of clients. Chief Justice King has indicated that the ultimate question is not whether the defendant's conduct accords with the practices of the profession, but whether it accords with the standard of reasonable care demanded by the law. That question is to be determined by the court and the responsibility for deciding it cannot be delegated to any profession or group in the community.[23]

In two of the handful of Australian decisions on information disclosure, medical evidence as to what constitutes acceptable medical practice was confirmed by the court. In the case F.v R., the plaintiff, who was pregnant with her third child, consulted a gynaecologist about sterilization.[24] Neither she nor her husband wanted more children. During the consultation, the husband raised the possibility of undergoing a vasectomy. The practitioner advised a tubal ligation but did not inform the plaintiff that there was a failure rate of less than one per cent. After undergoing the sterilization procedure, the woman subsequently became pregnant. Chief Justice King observed that the doctor would have been under a duty to disclose such information if the plaintiff had specifically asked about the possibility of subsequent pregnancy. He further commented that it would be better medical practice and consistent with the rights and interests of patients to warn of the slight possibility of a subsequent pregnancy. Nevertheless, failure to disclose was held to be in accordance with current medical practice and hence, not negligent.

In Battersby v Tottman, a mentally ill patient was prescribed excessive doses of a drug with known side effects, including retinal damage and consequent impaired vision.[25] The possibility of cardiac arrest was also adverted to by one expert witness. Only Mr Justice Zelling, in dissent, thought that a failure to inform a mentally ill patient of the risks of blindness and cardiac arrest constituted negligence. On the basis of these judgements, it seems likely that courts will not be prepared to override medical evidence except in the most blatant cases.

Whether the Australian High Court would choose to follow the Sidaway decision in preference to the above cases concerning information disclosure is not clear. It should be noted however, that since 1963 the High Court has chosen not to follow decisions of the House of Lords on a number of important common law issues.[26] In addition, the High Court has indicated on a number of previous occasions that evidence of customary or industry practices will not necessarily be conclusive on the question of negligence.

The reasonable patient test

Determination of whether adequate disclosure has been made is linked to the information needs of what a reasonable patient in the particular patient's position would wish to know.[27] A purely subjective disclosure test based on the needs of a particular patient has not been adopted in Australia. Such a test would require doctors to take into account the personal circumstances of the patient. Reluctance to impose liability on this basis no doubt rests on the assumption that practitioners cannot reasonably be expected to know the precise information needs of each patient, so that to require such a degree of knowledge would be to stretch the requirement of foreseeability to unreasonable limits. By subsuming an individual within the concept of the reasonable patient, negligence law permits idiosyncratic information needs and individual characteristics to be filtered out of the disclosure process.

A reasonable patient test may be more appropriate in cases of hospitalized patients receiving team care, and in some instances of specialist care where on-going, personalized relationships are unlikely. Despite the changing nature of Australian medical practice, close relationships between general practitioners and their patients are still possible. In these instances, a subjective standard of information disclosure is arguably appropriate.

The Canadian case Reibl v Hughes illustrates the application of the particular patient test.[28] In that case, the patient who suffered from carotid artery disease consulted the defendant about headaches. The patient did not appreciate that the surgery recommended by the defendant was to reduce the risk of a future stroke, and was not expected to affect his headaches. The fact that there was a ten per cent risk of a stroke associated with the operation was not disclosed. The patient was entitled to pension benefits if he continued to work for another eighteen months. After undergoing surgery, the patient suffered a stroke. The Canadian Supreme Court held that this risk should have been disclosed since, given all the circumstances, including financial matters, it would probably have influenced the patient to refuse surgery.

Exceptions to the duty to disclose

A common law duty to disclose is not absolute and does not arise in emergency situations, or where a patient waives the right to receive information. Discretion to withhold information is also permitted to practitioners in certain circumstances. A doctor may be justified in withholding information on this basis, if in his or her reasonable opinion, a patient's temperament or emotional make-up would prevent a rational decision. A withholding or a failure to volunteer information may also be justified where a doctor reasonably judges that "serious harm" to a patient's mental or physical wellbeing is likely to result.[29]

Chief Justice King has stated that a failure to disclose information may be consistent with a practitioner's obligation to act in a patient's best interests despite a specific request for information. This will be so when the patient's request springs from the desire for reassurance rather than for information. He cautioned however that a doctor "should hesitate long ... before withholding the full truth as to real risks of harm or failure when asked to explain them".[30]

Discretion to withhold information was canvassed in Battersby v Tottman.[31] Mr Justice Zelling, in dissent, argued that where the possible consequences are so serious, a patient must be able to make her own decisions, whether the doctor thinks she is well enough to do so or not. The only exceptions are in the cases of patients who are too young to make a decision or who, due to mental infirmity, are unable to appreciate the risks inherent in the treatment. In contrast to the majority, Mr Justice Zelling found that the plaintiff did not belong to this latter class.

Causation

As part of an action in negligence, a plaintiff must prove that failure to provide information caused injury. In essence, this amounts to a patient establishing that, if the relevant risks had been disclosed, consent to the operation would not have been given so that the injury complained of would have been avoided. A subjective test of causation has been adopted in some Australian jurisdictions which takes into account what the particular (as opposed to the reasonable) patient would have done if adequate disclosure had in fact been made.[32]

In Gover v The State of South Australia and Perriam, the patient consulted the defendant eye surgeon about her thyroid eye condition.[33] She was worried in particular about her left eye which she felt was "a bit starey". She also experienced redness in both eyes from time to time. The defendant decided to perform cosmetic surgery to reduce the fat across her upper eyelids. Following the operation, the patient developed trichiasis in the left eye and a related entropion. In the former condition, the eyelashes grow inwards whilst the latter condition involves a turning in of the lid margin. In addition, she was unable to completely close her eyes which in time could give rise to further serious complications.

The patient alleged that there was a foreseeable risk that these conditions would occur, and that the defendant was negligent in failing to warn her of all the risks involved, including blindness. Her plea was partially successful, in that the failure to warn of the entropion and trichiasis risks was found to constitute negligence. Because a risk of blindness was not known at the time of the operation, the surgeon was not held negligent in failing to warn the patient of this particular risk. The court applied a subjective test in relation to causation which the plaintiff failed to satisfy. On the basis that the entropion and trichiasis conditions could be dealt with quickly and easily, if they materialized, the court held that it was unlikely that the patient would have refused to undergo surgery, even if alerted to these risks.

AMERICAN COMMON LAW REGULATION OF INFORMATION DISCLOSURE

The doctrine of informed consent

Prior to the late fifties, the justification for disclosure and consent in the clinical relationship was derived from a beneficence model of health care, in which the primary obligation of physicians was to provide medical assistance. Well into the first decade of the twentieth century, the withholding of medical information from patients was commonly justified on the grounds of avoiding undue anxiety and concern.[34] In this model of medical care there was little room for notions of autonomy and patient choice. The late fifties witnessed the growth of interdisciplinary medical ethics together with the emergence of the doctrine of informed consent. The legal doctrine rapidly became the focal point of ethical debate concerning decision-making authority in the clinical and research relationships.[35] The developing case law reflected the changing political climate in its adoption of the rights rhetoric of various interest groups, including women and consumers.

The doctrine of informed consent is frequently associated with a trilogy of cases commencing in the late fifties. However, as early as 1914, Justice Cardozo in Schloendorff's case had emphasised a patient's right of self-determination in the following terms:

> Every human being of adult years and sound mind has a right to determine what shall be done with his own body: and a surgeon who performs an operation without his patient's consent commits an assault, for which he is liable in damages.[36]

At the time of this decision, which involved a battery claim against a medical practitioner, restrictive licensing and educational requirements had strengthened the power and prestige of the medical profession at the expense of alternative medicine. During the nineteenth century, the demise of alternative forms of medicine, and restrictions on the number of registered practitioners, significantly eroded patients' powers and choices. Against this background, Scholendorff and other decisions have been interpreted as an attempt by courts to maintain a balance in the clinical relationship against a rapidly expanding professional monopoly.[37]

In 1957, in the case Salgo v Leland Stanford Jr. University Board of Trustees, the plaintiff sued for the negligent performance of a translumbar aortography and for the failure to warn of a risk of paralysis. It was held that a practitioner was under a duty to disclose any facts necessary to form the basis of an intelligent consent.[38] Although the court was clearly concerned to ensure that consent had been informed when given, it nevertheless tempered its decision by stating that full disclosure should be consistent with the exercise of professional discretion.[39]

The issue which Salgo left unresolved was whether it was possible to reconcile early twentieth century cases, in which the obtaining of consent was treated as an aspect of good medical practice, with the Schloendorff line of cases, in which obtaining consent arose from an independent duty to respect patient autonomy and self -determination.[40] Nor was it clear, in the absence of any discussion of the legal basis of informed consent, whether the Salgo court regarded an action for the failure to obtain an informed consent as more appropriately framed in negligence or in battery.

Three years later, in Natanson v Kline, it was accepted that such an action was properly framed in negligence.[41] In this case, the plaintiff suffered severe radiation burns as a result of cobalt radiation therapy following a mastectomy. She claimed that the defendant had been negligent in administering the new treatment and in failing to warn her of inherent risks. The judgement endorses patient autonomy in language reminiscent of that of Justice Cardozo in Schloendorff's case. The court made it clear that although a doctor may believe a particular form of treatment to be desirable, the law does not permit the substitution of the practitioner's judgement for that of the patient. Whilst approving the ruling in Salgo, the court indicated that the adequacy of disclosure should be determined on the basis of the reasonable doctor test. In addition, it explicitly acknowledged that, in certain circumstances, the withholding of information is permissible on the grounds of therapeutic privilege. By permitting the premise of self-determination to be qualified in this manner, it is claimed that the court created "new tensions that have plagued the informed consent doctrine ever since".[42]

The adoption of a negligence framework left the courts with little room in which to develop a full-blown theory of patient autonomy. It is interesting that, despite the strictures of negligence, courts in the late fifties began to revive the concept of patient autonomy after it had lain dormant for so long. The reasons for this revival are not entirely clear. Jay Katz suggests that it is likely that judicial attitudes were influenced by advances in medical technology.[43] In both the Salgo and Natanson cases, the plaintiffs were exposed to serious risks arising from the diagnostic and therapeutic use of angiography and cobalt radiation respectively. With the increasing encroachment of therapy into the area of research, it is probable that the judges, prompted by the climate of civil rights, were no longer prepared to condone professional silence about risks.[44]

Other factors likely to influence judicial opinion were also at work. In 1966, the Surgeon-General of the U.S. Public Health Service (PHS) issued a policy statement requiring all institutions receiving PHS research funding to ensure that informed consent had been obtained from research subjects. An article published in the same year by Henry Beecher, a prominent medical researcher, documented a series of unethical research practices. Beecher's article aroused scientific and public interest and also influenced government regulatory policy concerning human subject research.[45]

A number of patients' rights statements were drafted during the seventies by various bodies commencing, in 1970, with the National Welfare Rights Organization. The most influential of these was published three years later by the American Hospital Association. Included in these statements was the right to make free and informed decisions. By acknowledging a patient's right to be included in medical decision-making and to make the final authoritative decision, these statements represent a revolutionary departure from notions of Hippocratic benevolence.[46] Their language and perspectives underscored an autonomy model of health care in which individuals are free to choose and act without constraints imposed by others.

During the seventies and eighties, there was a renewed interest in holistic and other forms of alternative health care. Included in the holistic theory of disease is the notion that an individual's autonomy can influence his or her state of health. Rediscovery of alternative medicine has been linked with judicial awareness that patient autonomy should be considered in terms of its effect on health. Martin Pernick suggests that "the malpractice-based standards of informed consent take into account the newly rediscovered impact of information, decision-making and autonomy on individual health".[47]

In 1972, against this background of events, the landmark case of Canterbury v Spence was decided. Its rejection of the paramountcy of professional judgement in determining the standard of care was heralded as a triumph for patients' rights. In the final analysis, however, much of the impact of the judgement is overshadowed by the confines of traditional negligence law.

Canterbury v Spence

The case arose as a result of the nineteen-year-old plaintiff agreeing to undergo a laminectomy for severe back pain.[48] He appeared to recuperate normally for the first day following surgery, but then suffered an almost immediate set-back after a fall from his bed. At the time of the hearing, he required crutches to assist in walking, and suffered from paralysis of the bowel and incontinence. The judgement echoes Justice Cardozo's earlier statement concerning the right of self-determination. Acknowledging the average patient's lack of medical expertise, the court indicated that true consent about what is to be done to one's body involves an informed choice premised on reasonable medical disclosure. The role of the physician is, therefore, to acquaint the patient with treatment options and any associated hazards. The ultimate treatment choice, however, rests with the patient.

The court explicitly rejected the notion that rules governing disclosure should be determined by prevailing medical practice. Instead, it reasoned that respect for a patient's right of self-determination demands a standard set by law. The extent to which medical custom was effectively ousted was immediately put in doubt by subsequent passages in the judgement. In characterizing medical decision-making, the court distinguished between those aspects for which medical expertise was essential and those for which it was not. Although a professionally determined standard of care was regarded as inappropriate for certain matters, the court stated that where professional judgement was called for, current medical practice was to be given its "just due". Despite the fact that the precise meaning of this term was not defined, the qualification nevertheless detracts from the affirmation of patients' rights contained elsewhere in the judgement.

Judicial ambivalence about the effect an acknowledgement of full-blown patient autonomy would be likely to have on professional judgement is evident in the manner in which the court defined the scope of the duty to disclose. Whilst acknowledging that the boundary of such a duty was shaped by the patient's right of self-determination and needs, the court was not prepared to impose a subjective test which would encompass a particular patient's information needs. Reasoning that this would place too onerous a burden on doctors, the court opted for the prudent patient test. Accordingly, a risk is material and must be divulged when a reasonable patient, in what the doctor knows (or should know) to be the particular patient's position, would be likely to consider it as significant. An important factor in adopting this standard was the belief that a plaintiff's testimony as to whether additional information concerning risk would have acted as a deterrent to consenting to treatment, would invariably be coloured by hindsight. Patient self-determination was further qualified by the defence of therapeutic privilege. Noting that discretion to withhold information as a matter of medical judgement could effectively destroy the duty to disclose, the court sought to limit its scope to situations where it is reasonably judged that divulgence would threaten the patient's wellbeing.

Canterbury has been acclaimed as an historically significant decision because it rejected the professional standard for disclosure already adopted in a majority of jurisdictions. In addressing the rationale for disclosure rules, the court examined the nature of the decision-making process. Diagnosis, risk identification and treatment options were characterized as matters calling for medical expertise. The decision as to which risks to undergo was a value judgement to be determined by the patient. Within the confines of negligence law, the Canterbury court, whilst falling short of an unqualified judicial endorsement of patient self-determination, nevertheless endorsed a patient's right to information. Although a correlative duty of professional disclosure existed in relation to such a right, in the court's judgement it was a right "which generated, rather than was subordinate to, the duty".[49]

Post-Canterbury developments

Prior to 1974, the doctrine of informed consent, as applied in a clinical context, was developed almost exclusively by the courts. In the next two years, a crisis in malpractice insurance, resulting from an increase in litigation and the size of damage awards, prompted a number of American States to enact informed consent legislation.[50] The legislation which was modelled on traditional negligence concepts, including the reasonable doctor standard of disclosure and an objective test of causation, was enacted with a view to curbing any rights of self-determination granted by the common law.[51]

The Canterbury decision appears to have been the high water mark of common law protection for self-determination and freedom of choice. Subsequently a number of courts chose to rely on the professional standard of disclosure.[52] As a result of this, and more particularly because of legislative initiatives, the role of the courts as instruments of change and development was effectively curtailed.[53]

The importance of American case law concerning the doctrine of informed consent is that it served as a catalyst for an ongoing inter-disciplinary debate which became the focus of an American Presidential Commission for the study of Ethical Problems in Medicine. In the following sections some major ideas and theories informing the current debate are outlined.

THEORIES AND VIEWS ON INFORMATION DISCLOSURE

Legal perspectives

According to certain legal perspectives, a right to receive information is an integral part of the social respect which individuals owe each other as community members. Recognition of individual autonomy is an essential component of this respect. In a medical context, respect for individuals includes recognition of a patient's interest in choice. This interest requires that patients are provided with all necessary information concerning risks, benefits and treatment options so that they can decide their own medical fate.[54] According to this line of argument, the requirement of obtaining patient consent is imposed "not in the interests of the patient's health, but in the interests of individual liberty".[55]

Legal scholars argue that information disclosure in the clinical setting should not be viewed as an exclusively medical matter, but rather as a process which offers freedom of choice and respect for patient self-determination.[56] Medical decision-making comprises technical and non-technical components. While diagnosis, prognosis, and the range of treatment options require medical expertise, a fully informed decision to choose or refuse a particular treatment is most appropriately made on the basis of a patient's own moral values, beliefs and preferences. Patients are equally competent to decide how much decision-making authority to vest in a practitioner.[57] Consistent with these views is the notion that professional judgement and expertise may assist, but should not override, a patient's right to make free and fully informed treatment choices, or refusals.

Because the common law fails to draw a distinction between technical and non-technical aspects of medical decisions, it has been criticized for giving insufficient recognition to patient autonomy and interest in choice.[58] Some argue, that by relying on expert evidence to establish acceptable medical conduct, courts permit professional judgement to determine what are essentially human rights issues. This, in turn, increases the likelihood that paternalistic arguments based on the avoidance of distress and patient inability to use information properly will be used to justify non-disclosure.[59]

It has been suggested that inadequate disclosure per se should constitute an actionable wrong. The basis for this contention is that the withholding of medical information constitutes an injury because the patient is denied an opportunity for free choice. Despite an absence of bodily harm, a patient's interest in choice is nonetheless interfered with, because failure to disclose is regarded as an injury to the dignity of the individual. Because the common law does not recognize this type of injury, it is argued that it affords insufficient protection to a patient's interest in free choice.[60] It is also contended that legal recognition of a dignitary interest of this nature, may encourage doctors to treat patients as their moral equals.[61]

A variety of legal solutions have been offered to ensure that patient choice is adequately protected. One proposal calls for an altered duty requirement necessitating disclosure of all relevant information concerning risks, benefits and treatment alternatives. This information, together with an accompanying professional recommendation, would enable a patient to make a free and informed decision. A determination as to whether the duty had been adequately discharged would not be made with reference to prevailing medical practice, but would involve a question of fact as to whether such information was disclosed.[62]

Infrequent litigation and the restrictive effects of precedent has led one commentator to reject common law solutions in an Australian context.[63] A preferred alternative is the enactment of legislation which would broaden the scope of the duty to disclose, and abolish the defence of therapeutic privilege. It is argued that difficulties in establishing causation could be avoided by categorizing a failure to disclose information as an actionable interference with a patient's right of choice. In addition, the implementation of communication skills training for doctors and patient and practitioner educational programmes are regarded as essential measures.[64]

Consumer perspectives

The consumer movement has long been concerned with the imbalance in decision-making power between consumers and traders. Recently, it has devoted a great deal of attention to the doctor-patient relationship where inequalities between the parties are partly attributed to the allocation of rights and duties at common law. Patients' lack of medical expertise and knowledge is felt to be of particular significance. Other important factors include a patient's gender, age, mental capacity, and ethnicity. Consumer groups have also drawn attention to shortcomings in the health care system including, inadequate practitioner training in communication skills and health insurance schemes which reward medical interventions rather than communication with patients. The restricted amount of time which practitioners are able to spend with patients in public hospitals, due to heavy work loads and inadequate staffing is viewed as an impediment to obtaining an informed consent. For these reasons, the implementation of disclosure legislation, together with patient and practitioner education schemes, is supported by a number of Australian consumer organizations. There is also a perceived need for additional informational aids, such as patient information sheets and, in the case of ethnic patients, interpreter services and translated materials.

Feminist perspectives

According to certain feminists provision of detailed medical information to patients does not satisfactorily address issues of autonomy and interest in choice. This is because discussions of risks, benefits and treatment options ignore the ideological contexts in which patient choices are made, as well as the social and medical implications of treatment.[65] Janice Raymond argues that invasive procedures such as transsexual surgery raise fundamental questions about free choice and the social and ideological appropriateness of these procedures. Further, she believes that classifying certain types of behaviour as warranting medical intervention, necessitates disclosure that not only conforms with legal criteria, but which also addresses the social and ideological implications of such intervention. By approaching effeminacy in men from a purely medical perspective, patients are not encouraged to see their desire as arising from the social constraints of role-defined behaviour. Consequently, a man who feels an instinct to nurture is encouraged to regard himself as female rather than as a male trying to discard his masculine role.[66] Raymond contends that a person seeking transsexual surgery must be made aware that within our gender defined society, medical intervention is the preferred approach. In essence, this means that when a transsexual's mind cannot adjust to societal roles, it is regarded as appropriate to adjust his body to his mind. Because surgical intervention replaces one sexual stereotype with another, she regards it as providing "a limited quick fix to the problem of gender dissatisfaction".[67]

The focus of the traditional informed consent debate is limited to the autonomy of the individual patient within the confines of the clinical relationship. As a result, Raymond argues that it ignores wider political and social contexts "which can undermine individual autonomy or competency".[68] Informed consent enhances autonomy by facilitating free choice. In the case of transsexual surgery, patient choice is limited to a medical procedure which promotes social conformity. Consequently, autonomy is actually "denied under the guise of fostering individual autonomy".[69] In order to adequately support free choice, information disclosure must include a discussion of the social and political contexts in which gender dissatisfaction arises and exists. Raymond contends that autonomy and free choice presuppose that a patient is presented with more than information about a range of available medical options. Legal and ethical dimensions of informed consent must also be considered, so that patients are made aware of the social and political consequences of medical treatment.[70]

Bioethical perspectives

In the previous chapter, Engelhardt's "peaceable community" was outlined as an example of autonomy-based ethical theory. In the "peaceable community," no one is entitled to subject another to a particular moral view without that other person's consent. The principle of autonomy demands a right to be left alone. This includes the right to be left alone in terms of one's choices.[71] In the absence of a common understanding or acceptance of moral authority, it is necessary to develop procedures which enable conflicting moral viewpoints to be mediated and, where possible, resolved. Engelhardt suggests that because individuals interact as moral strangers within the "peaceable community", rules are necessary to avoid misunderstandings and abuses of power.[72]

Similarly, in the health community, which is a microcosm of the "peaceable community", there is a diversity of moral views and no universally accepted moral authority. Although legal and professional standards define acceptable medical practices, there remains considerable leeway for discretion. Because of the impersonal nature of modern medicine, practitioners and patients will frequently interact as strangers in both a moral and technological sense. Consequently, prior to choosing a doctor, patients need to know the moral and professional ideals of practitioners and institutions. Equally, doctors need to know patients' expectations so that they can determine whether they are able to treat them, given their own values and beliefs.[73]

Engelhardt suggests that the justification for formal disclosure and consent requirements is twofold. First, they are necessary because mutual moral ideals cannot be assumed between practitioners and patients. Second, they offer some protection "against individuals imposing their understandings of the good life on unwilling others".[74] Informed consent rules should respect the freedom of both parties. Consistent with this principle, the purpose of informed consent is not to force patients to be autonomous, but to provide them with an opportunity to make autonomous medical choices. At the same time, such a principle would not permit doctors to be coerced into offering services they do not wish to provide.[75]

Covenant theory transcends the confines of legal rules by allowing parties to freely negotiate beyond the limits set by law. In accordance with this perspective, when a doctor believes that it is in a patient's best interests to receive full treatment information, he or she should have the right to make such a disclosure a condition of treatment, providing that this is made clear to a patient in advance. Equally, patients who so value self-determination that they are prepared to run the risk of possible harm resulting from disclosure should be free to make an agreement with a willing practitioner that they will be informed regardless of the consequences.[76] For proponents of covenant theory, the opportunity to come to a mutually agreeable decision on the allocation of decision-making authority allows patients, together with their doctors, to "realize ...their views of a proper patient-physician relationship.[77]

Medical perspectives

The traditional paternalistic model of medical care vests doctors with a considerable amount of moral authority and discretion on the assumption that doctors and patients equally value good health. According to this model, medical skills and experience are regarded as giving rise to an obligation to help patients, including taking responsibility for the choice of treatment, so that a practitioner who merely provides a patient with treatment options "is guilty of shirking his duty, if not of malpractice".[78] This assumption of responsibility is felt to be particularly appropriate in the case of acutely ill patients who, it is argued, are frequently reduced to a child-like state of dependency and therefore welcome being relieved of the responsibility of decision-making.

Supporters of the traditional model argue that, due to its complexity, patients will not understand, or be able to use, the information given to them by doctors.[79] It is also argued that providing this information may cause patients to become unduly anxious or overwrought. For these reasons, disclosure requirements are felt to be neither useful or important.[80] From a traditional perspective, demands for patient autonomy and freedom of choice threaten the trust on which the clinical relationship is founded. For some, an inevitable result of these demands is an unjustified inversion of roles with practitioners becoming the servants of their patients.[81]

For Jay Katz, both the traditional medical and the autonomy models of decision-making pay insufficient attention to interaction between the parties. Katz regards decision-making as a joint undertaking in which the nature and quality of the process is more important than disclosure of a particular risk.[82] He believes that the legal emphasis on risk disclosure makes obtaining an informed consent an event rather than an ongoing process, which does little to encourage patient participation and meaningful consent.[83] Katz contends that traditional professional notions of trust are based on a relationship which closely parallels that of parent and dependent child.[84] This type of relationship finds favour with practitioners largely because it pre-supposes "unquestioning compliance and unilateral trust on the part of patients". In turn, the nurturing role of the practitioner is welcomed by sick patients, particularly those who experience an accompanying regression to child-like functioning.[85] Certain assumptions and practices flow from this traditional view, including a belief that patients lack the necessary expertise to make decisions on their own behalf. This in turn has led to the assumption that practitioners should make decisions on behalf of their patients.[86] Doctors may manipulate and withhold information both to avoid conflict and ensure compliance with orders.[87] Because of these attitudes, patients have been deprived of information and thereby precluded from making meaningful treatment choices.

Restoration of health is a common aspiration of doctors and patients. Given the variety of options to achieve this end, agreement on which to pursue can only be achieved through conversation.[88] This necessitates the development of a new model of trust based on an understanding that the practitioner's role is to assist patients to make their own decisions.[89] This is best achieved by encouraging ongoing dialogue between the parties which may include investigating the reasons for consent to or refusal of treatment. The difficulties associated with patient choice, and the traditionally passive role of patients in medical decision-making, make it incumbent upon doctors to consider whether it is appropriate to interfere with patient choice.[90] A doctor's acquiescence in patient acceptance or refusal of treatment, without further investigation, is not necessarily respectful of patient autonomy. Rather, respect for a patient's psychological autonomy is compromised in these circumstances. Similarly, where a patient waives the right to receive information, doctors should not accept this abdication of decision-making responsibility without a concerted effort to discover the underlying reasons.[91]

Shared decision-making and the process of reflection is a joint endeavour. The introspective insights gained may alert patients to previously held misconceptions concerning their treatment or illness. Practitioners may discover that their unconscious treatment preferences have influenced patients to accept their recommendations, even though they had not consciously intended this result.[92] In this joint undertaking, the parties will confront anxieties and uncertainties, including scientific uncertainties. The acknowledgement of uncertainty by doctors will enhance the clinical relationship in a number of ways, including reducing "the exploitation of unwarranted certainty for purposes of control rather than care".[93] It may also reduce the feelings of abandonment on the part of patients caused by practitioners' silence or evasion as a result of uncertainty.[94] The concept of shared decision-making described by Katz seeks to enhance the autonomy of both parties by focusing on interaction and mutual dependence, rather than on an exclusive concept of either patient self-determination or physician discretion. He believes that his radically different model of decision-making can only be implemented by practitioner and patient education rather than by judicial, legislative or administrative orders.[95] In the final analysis, patients' willingness and capacity to make decisions will be contingent both upon their own efforts and the desire of practitioners to provide opportunities for reflection.[96]

Shared decision-making is by no means an exclusively medical concept. It is central to the beneficence in trust relationship described in the previous chapter and has been endorsed by an American Presidential Commission for the Study of Ethical Problems in Medicine. In its discussion of informed consent, the Commission looked beyond the confines of the legal model endorsing the notion of shared decision-making as follows:

> The Commission concludes that considerable flexibility should be accorded to patients and professionals to define the terms of their own relationships. The resolution favoured by the Commission is a presumption that certain fundamental types of information should be made available to patients and that all patients competent to do so have a right to accept or reject medical interventions affecting them. ... In the light of the disparities between the position of the parties, the interaction should, at a minimum, provide the patient with a basis for effective participation in sound decisionmaking.... It will usually consist of discussions between professional and patient that brings the knowledge, concerns, and perspective of each to the process of seeking agreement on a course of treatment.[97]

RECENT AUSTRALIAN DEVELOPMENTS

The need for additional information standards has been recognized by the Australian, New South Wales and Victorian Law Reform Commissions. In a joint report which rejected statutory provisions, the Commissions opted for the drafting of non-legislative guidelines by the National Health and Medical Research Council (NHMRC).[98] The Commissions stated that courts should continue to act as the final arbiter of reasonable conduct, but recommended that legislation should be enacted requiring courts to consider the guidelines when determining whether a doctor has acted reasonably in relation to the provision of information.[99] It was also recommended that relevant state legislation should be amended to provide that professional misconduct includes failure to provide adequate information about a proposed treatment or procedure.[100]

An additional recommendation stipulates that the guidelines should provide a basis for practitioner and patient education.[101]

Recently released NHMRC draft guidelines by a committee representing professional and consumer interests, reflect many of the theoretical perspectives and ideas previously outlined in this chapter.[102] The guidelines endorse the notion that, in order to make their own health care decisions, patients must be provided with adequate information which they are entitled to accept, or reject, free from coercion or undue influence.[103] Whilst acknowledging patient autonomy, the guidelines foster decision-making as a joint enterprise in which patients are encouraged to ask questions, and information and opinions are freely exchanged between the parties. The different types of knowledge which doctors and patients can contribute is deemed of equal importance for decision-making and patient well-being.[104]

Consistent with the approach taken by Jay Katz, the guidelines characterize providing patients with information as a process which may involve extended communication between the parties. The guidelines state that informed decision-making requires that patients are encouraged to reflect on opinions, seek additional advice, and consult with others before reaching a decision.[105] In addition to disclosing information concerning anticipated risks and benefits, doctors should fully explain the proposed approach to investigation, diagnosis and treatment and indicate whether the intervention is conventional or experimental. Patients should be made aware of the degree of uncertainty of diagnosis and therapeutic outcome. They should also be apprised of other options, the likely consequences of not choosing the proposed intervention, or of not having any procedure or treatment at all. An explanation of any significant long-term physical, emotional, mental, social, or sexual outcomes which may be associated with a proposed intervention should also be provided. The guidelines go beyond the common law in encouraging doctors to share uncertainties of outcome with their patients. The importance of this approach is stressed by Jay Katz who feels that a professional silence in the face of uncertainty creates a sense of alienation in patients. The guidelines are also in keeping with certain feminist points of view in so far as they stipulate discussion of the emotional, social and sexual outcomes of treatment.

Consumer groups and others argue that medical decision-making, particularly in a hospital context, is frequently impersonal with patients experiencing feelings of isolation and anonymity. The guidelines attempt to address these problems by providing that the identity, qualifications and expertise of those involved in the proposed intervention should be made known to patients. In addition, they state that the form and manner in which information is imparted should take into account the patient's circumstances, personality, expectations, fears, beliefs, values and cultural background.[106] Treating a patient as an individual with particular values, expectations and needs, which is characteristic of an ethics of care, represents a departure from the common law. The individualized approach of the guidelines whilst more demanding of practitioners, is clearly important given the multi-cultural nature of Australian society.

Withholding significant information is permitted under the guidelines in emergency circumstances, where a doctor reasonably judges that serious physical or mental harm might result, or where a patient waives the right to receive information.

In the latter instance, the guidelines stipulate that a doctor still has a duty to provide basic treatment information.[107]

OVERVIEW

The American doctrine of informed consent and the Australian common law of information disclosure were outlined above. Despite the more robust language of self-determination employed by American courts, the conceptual framework of negligence law common to both systems has resulted in roughly comparable decisions. In allocating decision-making responsibility between the parties, Australian common law oscillates between competing models of medical paternalism and patient autonomy. If the common law endorsed a purely paternalistic model of decision-making, practitioners would be vested with an exclusive right and responsibility to make decisions in the best interests of their patients. If, on the other hand, the law were to favour patient sovereignty, it would allow patients full responsibility and control for all decisions concerning their health. The locus of decision-making power in negligence actions does not reside permanently or irrevocably in either practitioner or patient. The negligence formula recognizes patient self-determination by permitting patients to waive their right to information. However, in certain circumstances, the defence of therapeutic privilege permits medical paternalism to override patient autonomy. Neither medical nor patient autonomy is exclusively favoured by the application of negligence law in relation to risk disclosure. Medical judgement as to what constitutes appropriate medical practice is subject to an overriding legal test, whilst patient autonomy is not measured by a particular patient's information needs, but is tempered by an objective standard of the reasonable patient.

There is now an emerging consensus, reflected in scholarly writings and the NHMRC guidelines, which characterizes patients as co-decision makers. Moreover, consistent with an ethics of care, it requires doctors to take account of the gender, ethnicity and values of each patient when discussing treatment issues. The reasonable person standard of the common law is becoming increasingly difficult to define due to the diverse nature of Australian society. The problem of devising laws for a multicultural society has been recognized by the Australian Law Reform Commission which is currently considering the adequacy of certain areas of law given the cultural and racial diversity of Australian society. One of the main purposes of this enquiry is to determine whether particular laws should be changed to respect and protect ethnic minority cultural values which are not currently taken into account.[108]

While the purpose of the common law is to devise standards which are adaptable to the changing needs of society, its effectiveness in the area of medical negligence is significantly reduced due to the dearth of litigated cases in Australia. In addition, the rapid advances taking place within medicine, together with the range of public responses which they have evoked, make it very difficult for courts to keep abreast of social consensus in this area. For this reason, the substitution of judicial for medical opinion as to what constitutes appropriate professional conduct is unlikely to yield standards which more closely represent prevailing social attitudes. One Australian judge has indicated, in an extra-judicial statement, that if the medical profession failed to take account of what the public required in terms of disclosure standards and perpetuated outmoded practices, "it would be the role of the courts in the individual case to apply a different standard".[109]   Given the mutual respect between the two professions, the trumping of medical expert opinion on these grounds is likely, in practice, to be an infrequent occurrence as indicated by His Honour's subsequent comment:

> A doctor is negligent if he fails to act reasonably in giving information and what responsible medical practitioners in similar circumstances do is an invaluable guide to the court when considering what the law requires unless there are good reasons to the contrary. One might expect logically that the case where there are good reasons to the contrary, given that we are blessed overall with a good competent medical profession will be exceptional and rare.[110]

The NHMRC working party guidelines on information disclosure display an admirable awareness of the various dimensions and components of medical decision-making. As such they will be a valuable supplement to the common law in fostering the general ideals of communication and trust between doctors and patients. If, as part of the information giving process, a more comprehensive and sustained dialogue is to be encouraged, the implications in terms of practitioners' time and the associated costs will need to be taken into account.[111]

If a lesson is to be learned from various movements, including the civil rights, women's and consumer movements, it is that any process of change which involves a fundamental re-evaluation of attitudes and values is not easily achieved. Clearly, one approach would be to implement information guidelines as statutory standards, with penalties for breach. This option is unattractive first because it runs the risk of creating an adversarial relationship between the parties. In addition, it creates problems in relation to policing and penalties. A preferred method of enforcing the guidelines is to amend relevant legislation governing medical practice so as to provide that failure to disclose adequate information constitutes professional misconduct. Because the aim of standard-setting in this area is to enhance communication between doctors and patients, all interested parties, including governments, must undertake measures to educate both patients and practitioners.

Notes

1. Informed Decisions About Medical Procedures. Report of the Victorian, Australian and New South Wales Law Reform Commissions, 1989, 7. (Hereinafter referred to as Informed Decisions About Medical Procedures.)
2. Informed Decisions About Medical Procedures, op.cit. 10-11.
3. Consent to Medical and Dental Procedures Act 1985 South Australia (minors); Mental Health Act 1986 Victoria; Mental Health Act 1983 New South Wales.
4. Informed Consent to Medical Treatment Victorian Law Reform Commission (Discussion Paper Number 7,1987) 1. The paper was issued in conjunction with the Australian and the New South Wales Law Reform Commissions. (Hereinafter referred to as Informed Consent to Medical Treatment)
5. Schloendorff v. Society of New York Hospital 211 N.Y.125, 105 N.E.92 (1914)
6. A recent case suggests however that there may be some cases in which consent will not be real even though the patient is aware of the general nature of the procedure. D v S. 1981 93 LS (SA) JS 405.
7. Chatterton v Gerson 1981 Q.B. 432.
8. Fordham J., Doctors' Orders or Patient Choice. Leo Cussen Institute 1988, 9; F v R (1983) 33 S.A.S.R. 189 at 192-3 (per King CJ.)
9. F v R, supra.cit. 191 (King CJ)
10. Id.92-3 (King CJ)
11. Sidaway v Governors of Bethlem Hospital and Others [1985]2 W.L.R.480, 491.
12. F v R, supra cit. 189, 191. (King CJ)
13. Id.191, 193 (King CJ)
14. Id.192.
15. Id.191.
16. Id.192-3.(King CJ); Gover v South Australia and Perriam (1985) 39 S.A.S.R. 543, 558 (Cox J)
17. Certain feminists put the argument more forcefully contending that the reasonable person standard is not gender neutral, but is male oriented. Bender L., A Lawyer's Primer on Feminist Theory and Tort. 38 Journal of Legal Education 1988, 3.
18. F v R, supra cit. 193.
19. Sidaway v Governors of Bethlem Royal Hospital and Others supra cit.491.
20. F v R, supra cit. 189,190 (King CJ)
21. Bolam V Fiern Hospital Management Committee 1957 1 W.L.R.582. I am indebted to Professor Sheila McLean for drawing my attention to the heavy reliance in the Bolam judgement on the Scottish case of Hunter v Hanley 1955 S.C.200., as well as to the following cases in which the decisions in Bolam and Hunter were held to represent Scottish, as well as English, law. Moyes v Lothian Health Board (1990) S.L.T 444.; Goorkani v Tayside Health Board 1991 3 Med.L.R.33.
22. F v R, supra cit. 194 (King CJ); Rogers v Whitaker 1991 Australian Torts Reporter 81-113.

23. F v R supra cit.194 (King CJ); Battersby v Tottman (1985) 37 S.A.S.R. 524, 537 (Zelling J)
24. F v R, supra cit.
25. Battersby v Tottman supra cit.
26. Informed Consent To Medical Treatment, op.cit. 16.
27. F v R, supra cit. 189, 192 (King CJ)
28. Reibl v Hughes (1980) 114 DLR (3d) 1, 10-11.
29. F v R, supra cit. 193. (King CJ)
30. Id.192.
31. Battersby v Tottman supra cit.534-5.
32. Gover v State of South Australia and Perriam (1985) 39 S.A.S.R 543,566 (Cox J); Ellis v Wallsend District Hospital 1989 Australian Torts Reporter 80 - 289.
33. Gover v State of South Australia and Perriam supra.cit. 543.
34. Faden and Beauchamp, op. cit. 84.
35. Id.86-7.
36. Schloendorff v. Society of New York Hospital 211 N.Y.125, 105 N.E.92 (1914)
37. Pernick M.S., The Patient's Role in Medical Decisionmaking: A Social History of Informed Consent in Medical Therapy. United States President's Commission for the Study of Ethical Procedures in Medicine and Biomedical and Behavioral Research. Making Health Care Decisions Vol 3. 1982, 30-1.
38. Salgo v. Leland Stanford Jr. University Board of Trustees, 317 P. 2d 170 (Cal. Dist. Ct. App. 1957).
39. Salgo v Leland supra cit. as cited in Faden and Beauchamp, op.cit. 126.
40. Faden and Beauchamp, op.cit. 127.
41. Natanson v. Kline, 350 P. 2d. 1093 (Kan. 1960).
42. Katz J., The Silent World of Doctor and Patient. The Free Press 1984, 71. (Hereinafter referred to as The Silent World.)
43. Katz J., The Senate's Definition of Voluntary and Informed Consent: Another View. 2 IRB: Review of Human Subjects Research 1980, 5-6.
44. Katz, The Silent World, op.cit. 63-4.
45. Beecher H.K., Ethics and Clinical Research. 274 New England Journal of Medicine 1966, 1354.
46. Faden and Beauchamp, op. cit. 93 -5.
47. Pernick, op.cit. 34.
48. Canterbury v Spence 464 F.2d. 772 (D.C.Cir.1972) In analysing this case the author wishes to acknowledge reliance on the ideas contained in Katz, The Silent World, op.cit.
49. McLean S., A Patient's Right To Know - Information Disclosure, the Doctor and the Law. Dartmouth Publishing Company 1989, 88.
50. For a summary of various statutory provisions and leading cases, see The United States President's Commission for the Study of Ethical Problems in Medicine and Biomedical and Behavioral Research - Making Health Care Decisions. Vol 3, 1982 204; see also Rosoff A., Informed Consent : A Guide For Health Care Providers. Aspen Systems Corporation Maryland 1981; Rodgers M.S., Legislating for an Informed Consent to Treatment. 26 McGill Law Journal 1981, 1056.

51. Katz, The Silent World, op.cit. 81.
52. Except for Scott v Bradford 606 P.2d.554 (Okla.1979) no decision expanded a patient's freedom of choice. Katz, The Silent World, op.cit. 80.
53. Faden and Beauchamp, op. cit. 139 -40.
54. Fordham J., Doctors' Orders or Patient Choice? Leo Cussen Institute, Melbourne 1988, 7.
55. Skegg P.D.G., Law Ethics and Medicine. Oxford, Clarendon Press 1984, 85.
56. McLean, op.cit. 26. The analysis in this section draws heavily on the arguments and ideas contained in this text.
57. Shultz M.M., From informed consent to patient choice: a new protected interest. 95 Yale Law Journal 1985 219,221.
58. In the American case Canterbury v Spence such a distinction was drawn. However as previously discussed, subsequent statements in the judgement appear to significantly qualify the distinction.
59. McLean, op.cit. 27.
60. Goldstein J., For Harold Lasswell: Some Reflections on Human Dignity, Entrapment, Informed Consent, and the Plea Bargain. 84 Yale Law Journal 1975, 683.
61. Meisel A., A "dignitary Tort" as a Bridge between the Idea of Informed Consent and the Law of Informed Consent. 16 Law, Medicine and Health Care 1988, 210,211.
62. McLean, op.cit. 172.
63. Fordham, op.cit. 51-2.
64. Id.51-64.
65. Raymond J., Informed Consent and Transsexual Surgery. Informed Consent Symposia, Law Reform Commission of Victoria 1986,44,47,49.
66. Id.47.
67. Id.47,49.
68. Id.47.
69. Id.48.
70. Id.49.
71. Engelhardt H.T., Free and Informed Consent, Refusal of Treatment, and the Health Care Team: The Many Faces of Freedom, in The Foundations of Bioethics. Oxford University Press 1986,250, 265-6.
72. Id.261.
73. Id.260.
74. Id.261.
75. Id.271,5.
76. Id.276-7.
77. Id.279.
78. Ingelfinger F., Arrogance. 303 New England Journal of Medicine 1980, 1507,1509; Siegler M., The Progression of Medicine - From Physician Paternalism to Patient Autonomy to Bureaucratic Parsimony. 145 Archives of Internal Medicine 1985, 713, 714.
79. Ingelfinger F., Informed (but uneducated) consent. 287 New England Journal of Medicine 1972, 465-6 as cited in Appelbaum P. Lidz C. and Meisel A.,

Informed Consent - Legal Theory and Clinical Practice. Oxford University Press 1987, 140.
80. Katz R.L., Informed consent - is it bad medicine ? 126 West J Med 1977, 426-28 as cited in Appelbaum, Lidz and Meisel, op.cit. 140,n.28.
81. Seigler, op.cit. 714.
82. Katz, The Silent World, op.cit. 83-4.
83. Id.82-3.
84. Id.100.
85. Ibid.
86. Id.83 ; Katz J., Physician - Patient Encounters "On A Darkling Plain." 9 Western New England Law Review 1987, 207,211. (Hereinafter referred to as On a Darkling Plain).
87. Katz, On A Darkling Plain, op.cit. 215.
88. Katz, The Silent World, op.cit. xviii.
89. Id.102.
90. Id.125.
91. Ibid.
92. Id.128.
93. Id.206.
94. Ibid.
95. Id.228-9.
96. Katz, On A Darkling Plain, op.cit. 215.
97. President's Commission for the Study of Ethical Problems in Medicine and Biomedical and Behavioral Research - Making Health Care Decisions Vol 1. 1982, 38.
98. Informed Decisions about Medical Procedures, op.cit. 23,28.
99. Id.29-30.
100. Id.31.
101. Id.26-9 .
102. General Guidelines for Medical Practitioners on Providing Information to Patients - Preliminary Discussion Paper. Report of the NHMRC Working Party on General Guidelines on Informed Decisions about Medical Intervention. Australian Government Publishing Service, Canberra. 1991.
103. Id. paras.5, 8.1, 8.2, 8.5.
104. Id. para.6.
105. Id. paras. 9, 11.2.
106. Id. paras.8.4, 9.
107. Id. para.12.
108. Multiculturalism and the Law. Australian Law Reform Commission Issues Paper No.9, January 1990 para. 11.
109. Judge Forno, Doctors' Lament or Informed Consent. Paper presented at the Tenth Conference of District and County Court Judges of Australia. July, 1989. 64.
110. Id.78.
111. Informed Decisions about Medical Procedures-Doctor and Patient Studies. Law Reform Commission of Victoria 1989, 59.

3 Refusal of Medical Treatment

INTRODUCTION

Death has always been a private affair in our society. As a result, it is avoided as a topic of everyday conversation. Recently, issues relating to death and dying, including refusal of medical treatment, have attracted a great deal of public attention. This is largely due to developments in life-sustaining medical technology which have prompted concerns that the dying should not be subject, in all circumstances, to heroic lifesaving measures. Many people are fearful that medical technology may be used to extend life, regardless of pain and discomfort. These concerns are graphically expressed by Paul Ramsey as follows:

> It is now possible to deprive many a patient of a fulfilment of the wish to have a death of one's own, the scene Dr Rynearson describes is one of patients with an "untreatable" disease being kept alive indefinitely by means of tubes inserted into their stomachs, or into their veins, or into their bladders, or into their rectums - and the whole sad scene thus created encompassed within a cocoon of oxygen which is the next thing to a shroud.[1]

Legal and ethical principles relevant to treatment refusal reflect patients' interests in self-determination, as well as countervailing State interests in preservation of the integrity of the medical profession and in preservation of life. Generally speaking, a patient is legally entitled to refuse any medical treatment and a doctor who disregards a competent patient's refusal by undertaking or continuing treatment will be liable in battery.[2] However, State interest in protection and preservation of human life limits a right of self-determination so that an individual cannot lawfully require another to assist him, or her, to commit suicide.

The question of whether refusal of medical treatment can amount to suicide has been the subject of extensive legal and ethical debate. A Victorian committee of enquiry which considered the issue noted that at common law, the following four elements are necessary to establish suicide: a) the person who intends suicide must actually die; b) the person must deliberately intend to kill himself or herself; c) the person must have caused his or her own death; and d) the first and second elements must happen simultaneously.[3] On the basis of this definition, the committee concluded that there is a clear distinction between suicide and the exercise of an individual's common law right to refuse treatment. Accordingly, a competent individual who refuses treatment which cannot cure, and which is burdensome, is not committing suicide. This is because a person, although desiring to be healthy once again, may nevertheless wish nature to take its course when treatment holds out nothing more than prolonged pain and suffering. The committee stated that "to die of a pre-existing illness or condition which cannot be cured, does not constitute suicide. Rather, a person is merely exercising his, or her, common law entitlement to refuse medical treatment".[4] Although suicide is no longer a crime in many jurisdictions, the Victorian Crimes Act 1958 provides that aiding and abetting another to commit suicide is a crime punishable by a maximum of fourteen years imprisonment. The legislation also provides that anyone may forcibly prevent an act of suicide, or the commission of any act which he or she reasonably believes may amount to suicide.[5]

According to ethical principles, as embodied in the Hippocratic Oath, doctors must work for the benefit of the sick to the best of their ability and judgement. A doctor's duty to incurable patients is to use his, or her, medical expertise to ensure their comfort, up to the moment of death.[6] However, this principle does not require the initiation or continuation of treatment which is of no benefit to a patient.[7] Respect for and interest in the preservation of human life is also the essence of the criminal law relating to all forms of murder and manslaughter. The deliberate killing of a patient is a criminal act, regardless of whether such an act is requested by a patient, or committed without his or her knowledge or consent.[8] Omissions, as opposed to positive acts, resulting in another's death do not, as a general rule, constitute murder or manslaughter. An exception to this is the legal duty in relation to the preservation of life. Such a duty arises when an individual undertakes care of a dependent person. It includes the provision of necessaries, which extends to medical care and treatment, as well as food and nourishment. Accordingly, doctors are under a legal duty to provide medical treatment to patients in their charge. If as a result of failure to discharge this duty, a patient's life is endangered, or his or her health impaired, a doctor may be charged with a criminal offence.[9]

Some commentators regard distinctions between acts and omissions as generally unhelpful.[10] According to Ian Kennedy:

> The real argument is not how a doctor's conduct can be characterized, but whether under the circumstances he has fulfilled his duty to the patient to care for him in good faith. The principles of good faith reflect professional ethics and general social morality. Neither at present condones euthanasia, so that, to cause the patient's death, whether by omission or commission,

would be a breach of the duty to care for the patient in good faith, and hence unlawful. Both, however, contemplate allowing the patient to die, if, under the circumstances, the illness is terminal and no other form of treatment, apart from treatment for dying, is ethically indicated.[11]

Public debate about death and dying inevitably has also included a considerable amount of discussion about active and passive euthanasia.[12] The distinction between these two forms of so-called "mercy killing" turns on whether a patient's life is terminated by an action such as the administration of a lethal drug (active euthanasia), or whether he or she dies as a result of an omission, such as failure to provide medical treatment, or nutrition and hydration (passive euthanasia).[13] The responses of Victorian doctors to a recent survey indicate that a clear majority support active, voluntary euthanasia.[14] In contrast, the Victorian Medical Board is strongly opposed to any legislation which could require the profession to practise active euthanasia for the following reasons. First, because such legislation would be against every principle for which the medical profession stands. Second, depression frequently accompanies severe illness which can affect an individual's competency to make such a request. Third, as there are no absolute certainties in medicine, no practitioner can be absolutely sure as to when an illness has entered a terminal phase.[15] The desirability and practicability of enacting legislation establishing a right to die was recently considered, and rejected, by a Victorian government committee of enquiry. In reaching its conclusion, the committee commented that an individual's right to die with dignity was not synonymous with euthanasia. Despite opinion polls to the contrary, it determined that, "legislation to cover "euthanasia" is not appropriate in Victoria".[16]

The case of Karen Ann Quinlan drew world-wide attention to treatment refusal in the case of incompetent patients. Important pioneering work in the development of guiding principles for treatment refusal was undertaken subsequently by a United States President's Commission. Throughout the eighties, American courts handed down a number of important decisions concerning the rights of competent and incompetent patients to refuse medical treatment. Not surprisingly, both in Australia and the United States, a broad spectrum of views was revealed in the ensuing public debate on the ethical and legal implications of these decisions. This debate prompted legislation in two Australian and thirty-eight American jurisdictions enabling individuals to make advance directives indicating the conditions under which they would want treatment terminated.[17] Federal legislation has also recently been enacted in the United States which is designed to encourage patients to formulate advance directives.[18] In contrast, the Victorian Medical Treatment Act 1988 attempts to protect patients from unwanted medical treatment by creating the offence of medical trespass.

In the following sections, significant American developments in this area are described, including recommendations of a United States President's Commission concerning treatment refusal, together with a number of land-mark American judicial decisions and recent legislative initiatives. Various theories are summarized and discussed with reference to some of these cases. Against this background of judicial, legislative and theoretical approaches, the Victorian Medical Treatment Act 1988 (as amended) is examined and discussed.

THE UNITED STATES PRESIDENT'S COMMISSION FOR THE STUDY OF ETHICAL PROBLEMS IN MEDICINE AND BIOMEDICAL AND BEHAVIORAL RESEARCH 1980-3

In its report, **Foregoing Life-Sustaining Treatment**, the Commission emphasised respect for the self-determination of competent patients in treatment refusal decisions and acknowledged that patients should have the ultimate authority to decide.[19] In the case of incompetent patients, the Commission recommended that a surrogate, usually a relative or friend, should make decisions on behalf of the particular individual. Surrogate decision-making should be guided by the principle of substituted judgement, which promotes patient self-determination and well-being. For patients who have never been competent, a best interests standard is preferred. This standard is defined, "by reference to more objective, societally shared criteria....[It] does not rest on self-determination but solely on protection of patient's welfare".[20] Routine resort to the judicial system should not be encouraged by courts or the legislature. Instead, the Commission stated that courts should ensure the appointment of appropriate surrogates vested with a range of discretions.[21]

The Commission indicated that decisions about life-sustaining therapy must be made in accordance with a patient's own values and goals. Because these decisions are rarely isolated choices, professional care-givers, together with friends and family, have an important role to play. Their presence, words and actions, contribute to the patient's assessment of the best course of treatment. In addition, their willingness and ability to carry out decisions often define a range of available options.[22] The Commission noted that health care providers are likely to be of most assistance to dying patients by "maintaining a predisposition for sustaining life (while accepting that prolongation of dying may serve no worthwhile purpose for a particular patient)".[23] The obligation to advise patients, so that they can make informed choices about life-sustaining treatment, is the same as in relation to other treatment decisions. Providers have an obligation to ensure that patients can choose from a range of treatment options, including that of no therapy. Because patients may associate a no therapy option with abandonment and unmitigated suffering, they should be made aware that supportive care will not be withdrawn as it is essential for a patient's comfort, dignity and self-determination.[24]

AMERICAN JUDICIAL DECISIONS CONCERNING TREATMENT REFUSAL

The role of the American courts in treatment refusal issues

Unlike their Australian counterparts, American courts are frequently involved in treatment refusal and termination issues. The relatively recent "institutionalization" of death, has been suggested as one of the reasons for American judicial involvement. As many as 80% of deaths in the United States, are estimated to occur in hospitals and long-term care institutions.[25] In Australia, approximately 65% of deaths take place in hospitals and allied institutions.[26] Because deaths occurring in institutions are subject to official scrutiny, any decisions made there are likely to attract public attention.[27]

This phenomenon is linked to developments in life-sustaining technologies and the rapid expansion of their availability and use. The total number of patients in the United States who are receiving life-sustaining treatment, either in the form of mechanical ventilation or nutritional support, has been estimated to be 3,775-6,575 in the former category, and 1,404,500 in the latter.[28] Given the capacity, and perhaps a tendency on the part of hospitals to sustain life, the ethical and legal implications of decisions concerning death have become matters of public concern.[29]

Other factors contribute to the frequent resort to courts in the United States. In many instances, health care facilities and/or medical teams responsible for treatment, find it morally unacceptable to comply with patients' wishes to terminate treatment.[30] Doctors and health care providers also fear litigation in the event of treatment termination. In addition, highly publicized activities of sectional interest groups, have polarized public attitudes about the use and discontinuance of life support systems.[31]

Patient autonomy

American courts have characterized the right to refuse medical treatment as a necessary element of an individual's right of self-determination. This right encompasses the notion of informed consent. In some instances, courts have also recognized a right of privacy as a basis for treatment refusals. This right is interpreted as including a right to be left alone and to be protected from government interference. It also includes freedom to make fundamental choices which involve an individual and his, or her, relationship with others, except where such choices are harmful to others and possibly to oneself.[32]

The right to refuse life-sustaining medical treatment is not absolute so that a right to self-determination will be recognized only if it outweighs all relevant State interests. The relevant countervailing interests which American courts take into consideration include, preserving life, preventing suicide, safeguarding the integrity of the medical profession and protecting innocent third parties.

Preservation of life

The law of most American states appears to endorse a competent patient's right to refuse treatment over state interest in keeping the patient alive.[33] In reaching its decision in In Re Conroy, the Supreme Court of New Jersey stated that, although there is a strong State interest in preserving life, it will not prevent a competent patient from declining life sustaining treatment.[34] This is because the life the State is seeking to protect is the life of the same person who has competently decided to forego the medical intervention, rather than some other actual or potential life that cannot protect itself.

In cases which do not involve the protection of the actual or potential life of someone other than the decision-maker, the State's indirect and abstract interest in preserving the life of the competent patient generally gives way to the patient's much stronger personal interest in directing the course of his, or her, own life. Indeed, in so far as "the sanctity of individual free choice and self-determination [are] fundamental constituents of life", the value of life may be lessened rather than increased by the failure to allow a competent human being the right of choice.[35]

Prevention of suicide

In cases not involving third parties, the court in In Re Conroy stated that the refusal of medical treatment should not be regarded as a suicide attempt, since it merely allows a disease to take its natural course. Hence, death is properly viewed as a result of the underlying disease and not as a result of a self-inflicted injury.[36]

Preservation of the integrity of the medical profession

Whilst recognizing an interest in preserving the integrity of the medical profession, the Supreme Court of New Jersey stated in In Re Farrell that health care standards were not undermined by a refusal of medical treatment in the circumstances of this case. Aware that a right of self-determination might conflict with professional ethics, the court commented that in the case of such a conflict:

> a patient has no right to compel a health-care provider to violate generally accepted professional standards. Cf. President's Commission Report, supra, at 44. ("A health care professional has an obligation to allow a patient to choose from among medically accepted treatment options... or to reject all options. No one, however, has an obligation to provide interventions that would, in his or her judgement, be countertherapeutic.")[37]

A similar limitation on a patient's right to refuse treatment was recognized in Brophy v New England Sinai Hospital.[38] In that case, the Massachusetts Supreme Court held that a patient in a persistent vegetative state could, through his family, refuse artificial hydration and nutrition. It further held, that the hospital need not remove the feeding tube which it considered would be contrary to professional ethics. Instead, the court required Brophy's family to move him to another institution which was prepared to comply with his wishes.

In contrast, Judge Compton, in a concurring opinion in the Bouvia case, discussed below, suggested that the right to die should include the ability to obtain assistance from doctors and others in making death as quick and as painless as possible.[39] This view places an absolute value on patient autonomy, so that doctors become servants of their patients. As such, it conflicts with theoretical interpretations of the clinical relationship based on a beneficence in trust approach or on a consensual form of decision-making. As Bouvia was a patient in a public hospital and not in a financial position to find alternative accommodation, her situation created a dramatic conflict between patient autonomy and professional integrity.[40]

Protection of innocent third parties

Courts have qualified a patient's right of self-determination on the grounds that the exercise of free choice could adversely affect the health, safety, or security of others. Consequently, competent adults have been required to undergo treatment against their will to protect the public health, or to avoid the emotional and financial abandonment of their minor children.[41] Courts have also ordered medical procedures to save the life of the pregnant patient's unborn child against the patient's wishes.

In one such case, a hospital sought an order to transfuse a woman who was thirty-two weeks pregnant. The woman, who was a Jehovah's Witness, opposed blood transfusions on religious grounds. The New Jersey Supreme Court granted the order stating that because the lives of mother and child were inseparable, it was appropriate to infringe upon the mother's wishes in order to give the child an opportunity to live.[42] In the case Re A.C., the District of Columbia Court of Appeals ordered a caesarian section to be performed on a twenty-five weeks pregnant, terminally ill woman against her wishes in order to save the life of the foetus.[43] The court subsequently reversed itself in a judgement which acknowledged that a woman's right of self-determination in such cases almost always outweighs the rights of the foetus.[44]

In the following sections, American cases concerning treatment refusal are discussed first in relation to the rights of competent patients. Cases dealing with the rights of incompetent patients are discussed subsequently under separate headings of once-competent and never-competent patients.

Treatment refusal by competent patients

In Re Farrell

In this case, Mrs Farrell became paralysed as the result of a nervous system disorder for which there is no available treatment or cure.[45] After the failure of a "last hope" experimental programme, she requested that she be disconnected from her respirator. Medical opinion confirmed that her decision was informed, voluntary and competent. Mrs Farrell died whilst still connected to the respirator. Nevertheless, because of the importance of the issue, the court agreed to render a decision.

In reaching its decision, the Supreme Court of New Jersey followed its previous decisions in the Quinlan and Conroy cases. Although the Conroy case involved an incompetent patient, the judgement included an analysis of competent patients' rights.[46] In Conroy, the court relied on the common law right of freedom from unconsented-to interferences, as a basis for the right to refuse medical treatment. In doing so, it expressly approved the principle of self-determination stated by Justice Cardozo in the Schloendorff case.

The court observed that the doctrine of informed consent was developed to protect a personal interest in bodily integrity. It also noted that ability to control bodily integrity through this concept becomes significant only when it encompasses a right of informed refusal. Reasoning that Mrs Farrell's right to live her remaining days as she chose, outweighed any interests which the State had in forcing her to undergo treatment, the court held that Mrs Farrell could choose to have her respirator disconnected.

Bouvia v Superior Court

In this case, Elizabeth Bouvia, a competent twenty-six year old woman, who had been rendered almost quadriplegic from cerebral palsy, sought removal of a nasogastric tube knowing that its removal would cause death.[47] In addition, she suffered from painful and degenerative arthritis, and was totally dependent upon others for her care. Because doctors believed that compliance with her wishes would violate their professional duty to preserve life, a feeding tube was inserted against her express instructions. Basing its reasoning on principles of self-determination and the right of privacy, the Californian Court of Appeal permitted removal of the feeding tube.[48] The court concluded that Bouvia was fully competent and entitled to refuse treatment, including that which may save or prolong life.[49] The court stated that a decision to refuse treatment is neither medical, nor legal, and properly belongs to a patient.[50] It added that there was no practical or logical reason to limit a right to refuse treatment to comatose or terminally ill patients. Noting that Bouvia's right to refuse treatment conflicted with the position taken by the medical staff, the court concluded that if such a right is to have any meaning, then it must be paramount to medical interests. It further observed that there was no State interest in preserving the life of a patient in Bouvia's condition:

> We do not believe it is the policy of this State that all and every life must be preserved against the will of the sufferers. It is incongruous, if not monstrous, for medical practitioners to assert their right to preserve a life that someone else must live, or, more accurately, endure for "15 to 20 years". We cannot conceive it to be the policy of this State to inflict such an ordeal upon anyone. It is, therefore, immaterial that the removal of the nasogastric tube will hasten or cause Bouvia's eventual death.[51]

The court rejected the State's competing interest in prevention of suicide as a reason to deny Bouvia's right to refuse treatment. Although Bouvia had previously expressed a desire to die, she stated in court that she did not wish to commit suicide.[52] Although the trial court found that Bouvia's refusal of treatment was motivated by a desire to end her life, the Court of Appeal held that there was insufficient evidence to support this conclusion. The court stated that it was clear that, as a consequence of her condition, Bouvia had resigned herself to accept an earlier death, if necessary, rather than be sustained by artificial feeding devices. As a result, her decision to allow nature to take its course should not be regarded as equivalent to choosing to commit suicide.[53] The court also rejected the argument that medical staff would be liable for aiding and abetting suicide if Bouvia starved to death while under their care. Stating that aiding and abetting involves a positive act, the court held that criminal liability is not incurred for honouring a competent patient's refusal of medical treatment.[54] The court stated that once Bouvia exercised her choice, a duty would nevertheless remain to provide appropriate treatment for alleviation of pain and suffering, unless such care was refused. Judge Compton, in a concurring opinion, held that the right to die is an integral part of our right to control our own destinies, so long as the rights of others are not affected. He further held that Bouvia was entitled to positive assistance from the medical profession in giving effect to her wishes.[55]

Treatment refusal by once-competent patients

In Re Quinlan

In this widely discussed case, twenty-two year old Karen Ann Quinlan became permanently comatose as a result of an intake of alcohol and drugs.[56] It was considered unlikely that she would regain consciousness or breathe without artificial assistance. Her father sought judicial approval to disconnect the respirator. Medical opinion suggested that this removal would not conform with professional ethical standards. Karen had not appointed a guardian nor made a living will. She had, however, intimated that she would not wish to live under certain circumstances analogous to her condition. In granting the relief sought, the court held that Quinlan had a Federal Constitutional right of privacy to terminate treatment. The court reasoned that if Karen were to be miraculously lucid for a moment, she would undoubtedly decide upon disconnection of the life support system. In addition, it suggested that countervailing State interests in the preservation and sanctity of life, as well as in the preservation of professional integrity, were diminished by Karen's extremely poor prognosis. The court commented as follows:

> We think that the State's interest contra weakens and the individual's right
> to privacy grows as the degree of bodily invasion increases and the
> prognosis dims. Ultimately there comes a point at which the individual's
> rights overcome the State interest.[57]

The court affirmed Quinlan's independent right of choice, which she could not exercise personally because of her incompetence. In these circumstances, the court stated that Karen's right of privacy could be asserted on her behalf by her guardian. Unable to discern her wishes from available evidence, the court adopted a form of substituted judgement, thereby permitting her guardian and family to exercise judgement on her behalf. The court order stated that if Quinlan's guardian, family and doctors were to agree that the life support system should be discontinued because Karen would not recover, they should consult with the hospital ethics committee. If that committee reached a similar conclusion, the life support system could be withdrawn and the doctors would be exempt from civil and criminal liability.

59

Following her removal from the respirator, Karen Quinlan survived for a further eight years without regaining consciousness. She died in 1985.

In Re Conroy

Mrs Conroy, who was resident in a nursing home, was incompetent and suffered from heart problems and chronic diabetes.[58] Her left leg was gangrenous and she was confined to bed and unable to move from a semi-foetal position. When she could no longer be fed orally, a nasogastric feeding tube was inserted. Her nephew, as her legal guardian, petitioned the court to authorize removal of the tube, contending that his aunt would never have agreed to its insertion. The trial court granted his petition, but its order was stayed pending appeal. Conroy died before the appellate court could rule, however the court decided not to treat the case as moot due to the importance of the issues which it raised. The decision of the lower court was reversed on the grounds that its order was an act of euthanasia. The case ultimately reached the New Jersey Supreme Court which held that the lower court was incorrect in ordering removal of the feeding tube and that the appellate court had erred in holding that removal of the feeding tube would constitute homicide. Although recognizing that a Federal right of privacy might apply, the court nevertheless based its decision on a common law right of self-determination and informed consent.

Reasoning that a right of self-determination should exist even if an individual is unable to sense that such a right has been violated, the New Jersey Supreme Court held that incompetent persons retain a right to refuse treatment. Provided one of the following three tests is satisfied, the right may be exercised by a surrogate decision-maker. Pursuant to the subjective test, a patient's wishes may be ascertained from available evidence, including oral statements or advance directives, such as living wills and enduring powers of attorney. Medical evidence of the patient's condition, treatment and prognosis must also be provided to the surrogate decision-maker. In order to give effect to a patient's right of informed consent, a surrogate decision-maker must have as much information on which to determine what the patient would have chosen, as a competent patient should have before deciding whether to accept, or reject, treatment. Such information may include present functioning levels, pain associated with the condition and its treatment, treatment options, and prognosis for recovery with, and without, treatment. The degree of humiliation, dependence, and loss of dignity resulting from the condition and treatment may also be included.

Where there is insufficient evidence of a patient's wishes, either of two "best interests" tests may be employed. The limited objective test requires trustworthy evidence of a patient's wish to refuse treatment coupled with a judgement that treatment burdens markedly outweigh the benefits of living. In the absence of information about a patient's wishes, treatment may be withheld or discontinued under the purely objective test, if it can be established that treatment burdens outweigh benefits and that continued administration would be "inhumane". When none of these tests can be satisfied, the court stated that it was best to err in favour of preserving life. The court made it clear that evaluation of a patient's life in terms of pain and suffering and possible enjoyment does not authorize decisions based on judgements about a patient's worth or social utility.[59] To further safeguard vulnerable residents of nursing homes like Mrs Conroy, the court held that termination and withdrawal of treatment decisions require the notification and participation of the Office of the Ombudsman for the Institutionalized Elderly.

In Re Cruzan

Nancy Cruzan sustained severe injuries in a car accident. Once it was apparent that there was virtually no chance of her recovering her cognitive faculties, her parents as co-guardians, sought and received authorization from a State trial court for withdrawal of artificial nutrition and hydration. The Supreme Court of Missouri reversed the lower court decision. Although the court recognized that a right to refuse treatment is embodied in the doctrine of informed consent, it rejected its application on the facts before it. It also declined to recognize a State constitutional right of privacy which would uphold the right of an individual to refuse treatment in every circumstance.[60] The court noted that Missouri living will legislation embodies a policy strongly in favour of preservation of life. Evidence regarding Cruzan's conversations with her housemate about her desire to live or die under certain circumstances were held to be inadequate to satisfy the statutory requirement of clear and convincing evidence of intention to refuse treatment. The argument that her parents were entitled to order treatment termination was rejected on the basis that no individual can choose on behalf of an incompetent person unless statutory formalities are complied with, or there is clear and convincing evidence of the patient's wishes.[61]

The matter went on appeal to the United States Supreme Court. Here the issue for determination was whether the State of Missouri was prohibited by the United States constitution from enacting the rules of evidence which it had concerning treatment refusal by incompetent individuals. The decision of the Supreme Court of Missouri was upheld by a majority of five to four judges.[62] The Supreme Court affirmed that a competent individual has a constitutionally protected right to refuse medical treatment, including lifesaving hydration and nutrition.[63] At the same time it was observed that this does not mean that an incompetent individual should possess the same right, since such a person is unable to make an informed and voluntary choice to exercise it. While Missouri law permits a surrogate to refuse hydration and nutrition on behalf of an incompetent individual, procedural safeguards had been enacted to ensure that a surrogate's action conforms as closely as possible to wishes expressed by the patient when competent:

> The choice between life and death is a deeply personal decision of obvious and overwhelming finality. We believe Missouri may legitimately seek to safe-guard the personal element of this choice through the imposition of heightened evidentiary requirements.[64]

The Supreme Court observed that procedural safeguards in terms of proof serve as a societal judgement about how a risk of error should be distributed between the litigants. A State may place an increased risk of erroneous decisions on parties seeking to terminate life-sustaining treatment. This is because an erroneous decision not to terminate maintains the status quo, and permits the possibility of a subsequent correction or mitigation either as a result of medical technology or the patient's unexpected death. In contrast, in the case of an erroneous decision to terminate treatment, there is no opportunity for subsequent correction. The Supreme Court added that the Due Process Clause does not require a State to accept the substituted judgement of family members in the absence of substantial proof that their views reflect those of the patient. It noted that there can be no automatic assurance that family views will necessarily be the same as the patient's would have been, had she been confronted with the prospect of the situation when competent. Stating that there was no doubt that the Cruzans were "loving and caring parents", the court commented that family members may not be entirely disinterested in their views. This is because they may not wish to witness the continuation of a loved one's life in what they regarded as hopeless and degrading circumstances. On the basis of the reasoning set out above, the court concluded that a State may choose to defer only to the wishes of a patient, rather than to entrust the decision to family members.

In their judgement the dissenting justices stated that, from a patient's perspective, an erroneous decision either way is irrevocable. While acknowledging that an erroneous decision to terminate will end in death, they argued that an erroneous decision not to terminate denies a patient the qualities protected by the right to refuse treatment. As a result, a patient will be forced to endure a degrading existence, whilst his or her family's suffering is prolonged. Such harm cannot be undone by a subsequent decision to comply with a patient's wishes. The dissenting justices also noted that, despite advance directive legislation in many States, evidence suggests that few people execute such documents. In these circumstances, testimony of family members and close friends is often the best indicator of a patient's wishes, since they are most likely to have discussed the issues with the patient. They concluded that a State may ensure that the surrogate decision-maker is the person whom the patient would have selected. It may also preclude individuals with improper motives from decision-making. Beyond this, a State must leave the choice to the party the patient would most likely have chosen as proxy, or allow the patient's family to make the decision.

Postscript

In August 1990, on the basis of new evidence from former workmates regarding Cruzan's wishes, her parents petitioned the lower court which had initially found in their favour. On 14 December 1990, the court ruled that there was sufficient evidence to satisfy the statutory standard of proof and that therefore the feeding tube could be removed. Nancy Cruzan died approximately two weeks later.[65]

Treatment refusal by never-competent patients

Superintendent of Belcher Town State School v Saikewicz

This case concerned a profoundly retarded, sixty-seven year old male who contracted leukemia.[66] Staff of the State institution in which Saikewicz was resident wished to treat him for his disease. Because he was incompetent and unable to consent to treatment, the institution petitioned the court for the appointment of a guardian. Those members of Saikewicz's family who could be contacted expressed no interest in attending judicial proceedings. The guardian's report indicated that Saikewicz's condition was incurable and that although chemotherapy was the appropriate treatment, it would cause discomfort and give rise to significant side effects. The guardian concluded that these factors, together with Saikewicz's inability to understand the nature and purpose of the treatment, and the fear and pain he would experience as a result, outweighed the limited prospects of treatment benefits. It was recommended that it would be in Saikewicz's best interests not to treat. This recommendation was confirmed by the judge at first instance. The matter went on appeal to the Supreme Court of Massachusetts.

At the time of the appeal, apart from his leukemia, Saikewicz enjoyed good health, was physically strong, well nourished and ambulatory. Although unable to talk, he conveyed his intentions by a series of gestures and grunts. The following factors were included in the findings of the judge at first instance: 1) Evidence suggested that if Saikewicz received chemotherapy, he would have a 30% to 40% chance of a remission from two to thirteen months. Without treatment, his life expectancy would range between a matter of weeks to several months, with the likelihood of a relatively painless death. 2) Despite severe side effects accompanying chemotherapy, most people choose to undergo treatment rather than let the disease run its natural course. 3) The administration of chemotherapy requires co-operation over several weeks which Saikewicz would be unable to give because of his retardation. 4) Although it is impossible to predict how long he would live with or without treatment, it is highly likely that he would die sooner without treatment than with it. The judge decided against permitting treatment on the basis of Saikewicz's age, his inability to cooperate, the suffering and side effects associated with treatment, the low chance of remission, and the quality of life possible, even if remission were to occur.

The Massachusetts Supreme Court relied on a right of privacy and a right of informed consent to permit withholding of treatment. In reaching its decision, the court held that a right to refuse treatment extends to incompetent as well as competent individuals. The court identified a number of countervailing State interests, including preservation of life, protection of innocent third parties, prevention of suicide, and maintenance of the integrity of the medical profession. The court recognized the first of these interests as paramount, suggesting that it was greatest when illness was curable, "as opposed to the State interest where, as here, the issue is not whether, but when, for how long, and at what cost to the individual that life may be briefly extended".[67] The court added that recognition of a right to refuse treatment in appropriate circumstances is consistent with medical mores, and does not threaten the integrity of the profession or the State's interest in protecting life.

The court employed a substituted judgement test to determine Saikewicz's wants and needs. This standard was defined as the making of a decision which would be made by the incompetent person if that person were competent, taking into account present and future incompetence as a factor which would necessarily enter into the competent individual's decision. The court noted that when applying substituted judgement, inquiry into what a majority of people would do in similar circumstances incorporates an objective element. Acknowledging the value of indirect evidence of this nature, the court observed that the test is nevertheless, a subjective one. Its aim is to determine the wants and needs of the particular individual involved, which may not conform to what most people regard as wise or prudent. The court acknowledged the difficulty of determining Saikewicz's wants and needs due to his profound retardation, inability to communicate, and the significant period of his institutionalization. It observed that a greater degree of reliance on objective criteria would therefore be necessary than is required in the case of a once-competent individual with established family relationships such as Karen Quinlan. Despite these difficulties, the court stated that the standard should not be abandoned because of the respect it accords to individual integrity and autonomy.

The court held that evidence which suggested that most people choose to undergo treatment had no bearing on the choice Saikewicz would be likely to make as he lacked understanding of his condition and prognosis. In order to make a worthwhile comparison the court reasoned that:

> one would have to ask whether a majority of people would choose chemotherapy if they were told merely that something outside of their previous experience was going to be done to them, that this something would cause them pain and discomfort, that they would be removed to strange surroundings and possibly restrained for extended periods of time, and that the advantages of this course of action were measured by concepts of time and mortality beyond their ability to comprehend.[68]

The court concluded that an important factor to be considered in applying the substituted judgement standard was Saikewicz's inability to co-operate with the treatment. Evidence suggested that Saikewicz would be unable to comprehend the disruptive effects of treatment on his stable and secure environment. Moreover, the possibility that he would need to be restrained during treatment might serve only to increase his fears, and possibly affect his ability to withstand toxic side effects of the chemical treatment. The court noted that the judge at first instance had identified quality of life as one of the factors weighing against treatment. The court made it clear that any attempt to value an individual's life was not permissible. It suggested that the manner in which the lower court used the phrase should be interpreted as a reference to the continuing state of pain and disorientation brought about by the treatment. As such, it was consistent with a decision based on Saikewicz's actual interests and preferences. The court concluded that responsibility for such a decision was properly vested in the judiciary, and should not be entrusted to any other group purporting to represent the conscience and morality of society.

In Re Storar

John Storar, a fifty-two year old profoundly retarded male, developed cancer of the bladder.[69] When the hospital authorities would not administer radiation therapy without guardian consent, his mother applied to the court and was appointed his guardian. Subsequently, with her consent, radiation therapy was administered for six weeks. After a temporary remission, his condition was diagnosed as terminal and his life expectancy was estimated at from three to six months. Mrs Storar agreed to permit blood transfusions. These were undertaken for several weeks until she requested that they be discontinued. The director of the centre where Storar was resident sought court authorization to continue the transfusions, arguing that death would otherwise occur within weeks. Mrs Storar cross-petitioned for an order prohibiting the treatment. The court appointed a guardian ad litem and made an order for continuation of the transfusions, pending the outcome of the hearing.

Evidence before the court suggested that Storar found the transfusions disagreeable and was distressed by blood in his urine which increased immediately following such a procedure. He did not understand their purpose and had displayed some initial resistance on one or two occasions. This resulted in sedation to relieve his pain and apprehension. Mrs Storar wanted to stop the treatment so that her son would be comfortable. She was unable to determine if he wished to live, but because of his attitude to the treatment, she believed that he would want it discontinued. She admitted that nobody had explained to her what might happen if the transfusions were stopped. The court held that the application to continue the transfusions should be denied. The right of an incompetent individual to refuse treatment may be exercised by another. In this case, Mrs Storar was best placed to determine her son's interests and she wanted his suffering to stop, believing that this is what he also wanted.

On appeal, the New York Court of Appeals declined to base a right to refuse treatment on a constitutional right of privacy. Instead, it found that such a right was adequately supported by the doctrine of informed consent. Implicitly rejecting the approach taken in the Saikewicz case, the court stated that, because Storar had never been competent, it would be unrealistic to attempt to determine whether he would choose to continue treatment, if competent. Instead, the court held that in assessing his rights, it was appropriate to place him in the legal category of an infant. In granting an order for the transfusions, the court held that although parents or guardians have the right to consent to medical treatment on behalf of an infant, they may not deprive a child of life saving treatment. An incompetent patient should not be allowed to bleed to death, despite family feelings that this is in a patient's best interests.

THEORIES AND VIEWS ON REFUSAL OF TREATMENT ISSUES

Medical perspectives

An ethics of responsibility

Patricia Powell suggests that medical decision-making can be enhanced by linking an ethics of responsibility (or care) with an ethics of rights.[70] Powell believes such an approach is particularly appropriate when considering the withholding of treatment from never-competent individuals.[71] Of fundamental importance to this ethical model is respect for individuals which requires not only that we avoid harming others, but also that we nurture their capacities for autonomy and relationship. Communication founded in trust together with a "process of loving attention" are essential for determining an individual's capacities in this regard. This process involves striving to understand all relevant aspects of a patient's experience.[72] It also requires that we relate to others as they are and not as we would like them to be. Information gleaned from intimate attachments between people enables decision-making to be tailored to the needs of each individual. According to an ethics of responsibility, moral choice should not be determined solely by the application of abstract principles. Rather, objective rules must be tempered with subjective knowledge gained from a "process of loving attention". It is this subjective information concerning the ethical, emotional and personal needs of a patient which Powell believes is essential in treatment termination decisions.[73]

An ethics of responsibility focuses on links and relationships between people uniting individuals in a common cause of caring for a patient. Within this framework, responsibility is not perceived of as an obligation which may be demanded as of right. Instead, it is regarded as arising out of membership of the community.[74] According to this ethical approach, all patients are owed care and respect regardless of whether they are capable of acting autonomously or of relating to others. Patients lacking autonomy and a capacity for relationships with others who suffer from a fatal illness, and patients who cannot be expected to significantly improve and for whom treatment causes substantial pain, should not be forced to undergo painful procedures to extend life. A moral decision may be taken for these patients to provide comfort rather than cure. Such a decision does not imply abandonment or the withdrawal of all treatment.[75] Powell argues that maximizing autonomy for incompetent patients, which is characteristic of an ethics of rights, is a harmful fiction because it leads to the isolation of dependent patients. At the same time, it distracts others from attempting to understand the responsibilities owed to vulnerable individuals.[76]

From an ethics of responsibility perspective, the adversarial process is an unsuitable means of resolving treatment refusal issues, because it destroys trust, hinders communication and prevents a focusing of attention on the patient. The threat of possible litigation is counter-productive to what Powell perceives as appropriate decision-making, because parties become concerned with their legal vulnerability instead of the patient's welfare.[77] Whilst not dispensing entirely with judicial determination, she would limit recourse to the courts as a means of resolving treatment refusal issues.[78]

Application of an ethics of responsibility to the Storar decision

Powell argues that by assessing Storar's rights as though he were an infant, the court turned away from the patient as he really was and ignored information unique to his situation. She is critical of this approach because the limits to Storar's capacities were not temporary. Further, cases involving the transfusion of infants against the religious-based wishes of their parents are distinguishable from Storar's situation because in those cases the transfusions were curative. As a result of the transfusions, the infants had the potential to live normal lives. For Storar, however, the treatment offered no cure and could not carry with it the opportunity for future autonomy.[79] The judge sought to protect Storar's autonomy, a capacity which he clearly lacked. Such an approach, while consistent with a rights perspective, is clearly at odds with an ethics of responsibility. Moreover, the judge failed to respond to Storar's actual qualities and instead responded to those which he would have liked Storar to possess. Powell suggests that the decision might be appropriate for an otherwise healthy infant or a once-competent adult, but not for someone like Storar.[80]

Judge Wachtler not only failed to pay sufficient attention to Storar's particular circumstances, but also failed to recognize how subjective information may undermine the appropriateness of rules.[81] Powell argues that Storar had no way of understanding the significance of his treatment. Moreover, she contends that because of "extreme bewilderment" and "subtle changes in his state", his level of pain was considerably more than acknowledged by the court.[82] In contrast, Judge Jones, in his dissenting judgement, noted Storar's increasing discomfort and hostility, which necessitated the use of physical restraints during transfusions. Unlike the majority, Judge Jones concludes that Storar did not function at his "usual level". He also found that although still capable of bathing himself, he became more withdrawn and ventured infrequently outside his room. Powell also finds the judgement lacking because the court failed to take account of the changing nature of Storar's condition with the result that no limitations were placed upon the order to transfuse. The implication of this, she contends, is that there is no point at which comfort is an acceptable goal of treatment.[83]

For Powell, the judgement illustrates the inadequacy of a rights-based approach to decision-making. The court attempted to protect Storar's rights but as Storar was incapable of exercising any rights, the effect of the decision was to prevent his mother making a decision on his behalf. The result was a brief extension of a life which was both painful and confusing.[84] Storar was capable of forming relationships and of placing his trust in others. That trust and sense of security was destroyed before he died. So too was Mrs Storar's sense of protectiveness towards her dying son. Powell believes that the dignity of dying or severely ill incompetent patients is best protected by incorporating the norms of the ethics of responsibility into medical decision-making. Such an approach favours responding to their need for comfort and communication rather than technological intervention when cure is impossible.[85]

Legal perspectives

Rules v relationships

Susan Wolf argues that the Missouri court's decision in the Cruzan case represents the gulf between a society shaped by legal formalism and abstract rules, in which people communicate like lawyers, and a society in which relationships play a major role in interpreting individual needs and preferences.[86] According to Wolf, the issue is not whether one individual's right of self-determination may be exercised by another, as there was sufficient evidence of Nancy's preferences to enable a decision to be made based on her wishes. The Missouri procedural requirements and evidentiary burdens threaten self-determination because of the difficulty of satisfying these standards. Because the statutory standards demand so much formality and specificity, compliance becomes well nigh impossible. As a result, the right disappears.[87]

In most jurisdictions, with the exception of New York and Missouri, courts have been willing to allow surrogates to determine a patient's preferences based on intimate knowledge and prior statements. By rejecting the family's evidence and role, Wolf suggests that the court endorsed a world in which relationships have no value and people talk of death in legal terms. The result is that Nancy Cruzan's fate was determined according to rules which "err on the side of life" but which had nothing to do with her particulars.[88] Acknowledging that the judgement aims to protect incompetent individuals from abusive and erroneous family decisions, she points to existing institutional and statutory safeguards designed to challenge unscrupulous decision-making. For this reason, she believes that there are no satisfactory grounds for denying the existence of family relationships and for rejecting intimate family knowledge of a patient. Moreover, what happens to one's body is so personal that it should not be left to strangers to determine, according to impersonal legal rules.[89]

Caring and justice - an institutional approach

Larry Palmer argues that lawmakers should focus on the social and organizational dimensions of medical issues rather than on individual doctor-patient relationships. Such an approach is warranted because medicine does not merely encompass the activities of healthcare professionals but is also a formal institution within society. Law should regulate the institutional structure of medicine with a view to encouraging health care organizations to develop their own regulatory systems so that recourse to law is necessary only as a last resort.[90]

Palmer rejects informed consent as the moral and ethical basis of legal decision-making arguing that an emphasis on self-determination for seriously physically, or mentally, ill patients leads to psychological isolation of those most in need of care. Like Jay Katz, he believes that doctors must share with patients the inherent uncertainties of medicine. The current emphasis on informed consent, he suggests, glosses over certain assumptions about medical expertise and patient knowledge and comprehension which warrant further consideration.[91] The institutional approach rejects the idea that the imagined will of a critically ill patient is the ultimate source of moral authority for treatment decisions. Instead, it acknowledges that these patients are entitled to care, regardless of whether medical intervention is involved. Care in this context is defined to include social connections and a sharing of the patient's pain, ambivalence and silence.[92]

Palmer finds judicial attempts to resolve ethical issues concerning the critically ill unsatisfactory. The decided cases have not given rise to a consensus on procedural and substantive issues. Palmer suggests that a bare legal endorsement of a right of self-determination does not provide caring or justice for a critically ill institutionalized patient.[93] A focus on the adequacy of proof concerning a patient's wishes about treatment withdrawal ignores the role of caring and compassion in tending to the critically ill. Consequently he contends that courts must discover the manner of discourse about caring which includes non-verbal communication. Law should not assume when patients refuse treatment, or do not express a preference, that they also wish to forego care.[94]

Palmer also notes that judicial analysis is limited in so far as it ignores the institutional context of medical decisions.[95] He reminds us that the social fabric of society influences the way in which its members die. In the face of medical technology, there is a preoccupation with quick and painless death. He cautions that unless we develop social structures to deal with anxieties about death, we are likely to inflict death on others as protection from our own anxieties.[96] He believes that law should encourage medicine not only to concern itself with cure, but also with allowing death to occur in a morally acceptable fashion. This will entail hospitals assuming responsibility for developing ways of caring for the critically ill, together with the development of an independent hospice programme.[97] The importance of such an initiative is that it provides a social context in which it is morally acceptable for patients to die and which provides them and their loved ones with the necessary support.[98]

Application of an institutional perspective to the Saikewicz decision

Palmer argues that recourse to the law was not so much a search for greater wisdom as an attempt to apportion responsibility for caretaking functions between law and medicine. A central issue was the caretaking function of institutions for the intellectually disabled. He argues that the outcome was determined in part by the fact that Saikewicz needed to be hospitalized for treatment. Moreover, his primitive form of communication, coupled with a possible need for physical restraint, put him at odds with professional notions of the good patient. In short, Saikewicz's problem was that he required too much care. Medicine's caretaking function presupposes other support mechanisms which were lacking for Saikewicz because his family expressed no interest in his welfare. Palmer believes that this lack of support may explain why the court rejected treatment for Saikewicz.[99]

Bioethical perspectives

Beneficence in trust

According to a beneficence in trust model of decision-making, the good of competent patients is best served when they decide what care to receive or refuse. Patient choice should only be limited if it would result in harm to others, or if compliance would violate a doctor's conscience. Biomedical good and medical indications may not override the higher good of patient choice.[100] In the case of incompetent patients, doctors incur a special moral obligation to ensure that their wishes are observed.

Because conflicting interpretations of a patient's wishes are likely, the following guidelines were devised to help resolve such conflicts.[101]

Doctors as surrogate decision-makers and advocates

Where a patient has not executed an advance directive, a doctor must consult with those parties who are best placed to determine a patient's wishes. Beneficence in trust vests doctors with a responsibility to determine whether a surrogate is making a morally acceptable judgement.[102] In the absence of both a morally valid surrogate and advance directive, a doctor assumes the potentially conflicting roles of expert, advocate and surrogate. Where information about the personal values of an incompetent patient is lacking, medical good is the only level of good which is ascertainable. Treatment decisions must however include a calculation of a patient's presumed or probable values. This calculation should be guided by a principle of beneficence in trust, so that any proposed treatment must provide some benefit, as well as being effective. Treatment burdens should not outweigh expected benefits. While a patient's physical and existential condition is relevant to these calculations, estimates of social worth are not. Acts of "therapeutic belligerence," such as sustaining life in all circumstances, are also excluded from these calculations.[103]

Responsibility for decision-making

Beneficence in trust requires that patients' values and preferences should form the basis of negotiation and dialogue and must not be overridden in any treatment plan. If patient and practitioner values conflict, the parties are free to withdraw. In preference to stressing individual freedom at the expense of moral values in medicine, the life-affirming values of the medical profession should be emphasised. These values should serve as a basis for dialogue as well as affording protection to those practitioners who object to assisted suicide.[104] A judicial determination should be sought only when a decision as to what is in a patient's best interests cannot be determined according to an advanced directive, the decision of a surrogate, or by a doctor acting in a surrogate capacity.

Application of beneficence in trust perspective to the Bouvia decision

In the Bouvia case, patient autonomy is interpreted as an absolute right. Pellegrino and Thomasma suggest that gains from such an approach include an enhanced sense of freedom and social respect for, and acceptance of, patient rights, particularly for the rights of the especially vulnerable. Against this they contend that the respect and mutuality of the doctor-patient relationship may be irreparably damaged. The integrity of the profession in their commitment to their patients' welfare and perhaps their right to withdraw are demeaned. According to this perspective, Judge Compton's decision reduces the role of doctors to that of agents and implies that the next logical step is to endorse euthanasia on demand. Beneficence in trust affirms the right to refuse treatment in the circumstances of the Bouvia case. This approach does not permit a patient to require doctors to co-operate in an action which they deem immoral. Accordingly, Bouvia was initially entitled to refuse the insertion of the tube. The authors contend that, once in place, its removal cannot be condoned, since the intent would be to cause death. Even if the tube were to be forcibly inserted, as happened in the Bouvia case, a beneficence in trust perspective would not permit its subsequent removal.[105]

Application of beneficence in trust perspective to the Quinlan decision

Pellegrino and Thomasma believe that if a beneficence in trust model were to be applied in the Quinlan case, it would not result in a radically different outcome. A patient's own assessment of her welfare, and her inherent dignity as an individual to express her wishes, take precedence over medical good. Quinlan's wishes were clear and were voiced by her family in a credible manner. Continuation of her life support system in these circumstances would constitute a violation of her humanity. Beneficence in trust does not require that life must be sustained where prognosis is hopeless. Further clarification or consultation, as recommended in Quinlan, is unnecessary if a prognosis is well substantiated, and a patient's wishes are properly represented by a morally valid surrogate decision-maker.[106]

Application of a beneficence in trust perspective to the Saikewicz decision

Pellegrino and Thomasma argue that in this case the use of a substituted judgement standard was inappropriate as Saikewicz's values and preferences could never be known as required by the beneficence in trust model. Substituted judgement as applied by the court was in effect a quality of life judgement. This violates beneficence in trust. The authors suggest that in such cases a medical indications standard is more appropriate. This standard does not require treatment in all circumstances, and only treatments that are effective and beneficial can be presumed to be in the patient's best interests. A patient should be treated where it is determined that some benefit outweighs the harms and burdens.[107]

RECENT AMERICAN LEGISLATIVE DEVELOPMENTS

The Patient Self-Determination Act 1990, which became effective on December 1, 1991, is the first Federal statute concerning advance directives and the right to refuse life-sustaining medical treatment. The legislation applies to all health care institutions receiving Medicare and Medicaid funds, including hospitals, nursing facilities, hospices, home health agencies and pre-paid health care organizations. The aim of the legislation is to encourage, but not require, the formulation of advance directives both to improve communications between patients and doctors and to ensure that a patient's expressed wishes are observed.[108] To this end, all relevant institutions must provide written information to patients at the time of their admission concerning an individual's right under State law to make decisions about medical care, including treatment refusal and the formulation of advance directives. Patients must also receive written information detailing institutional policies regarding the implementation of such rights. An individual's medical record must indicate whether or not an advance directive has been executed. Institutions are required to comply with State law concerning advance directives and must not make care conditional upon the execution of an advance directive. In addition, institutions must educate staff and the community on issues concerning advance directives. The Act also imposes obligations on States to prepare written descriptions of relevant laws to be distributed to patients on admission. Finally, the secretary of DHHS is required by the legislation to assist with the development of materials and undertake a public education campaign.

AUSTRALIAN DEVELOPMENTS - VICTORIAN LAW

Australian courts are resorted to relatively infrequently in matters arising out of treatment refusals. This is in sharp contrast to the American situation where courts have assumed a major role in shaping medical decision-making in this area.[109] Instead, regulation in this area has taken the form of statutory standards.[110]   A specially-appointed Victorian government committee which considered alternative methods of regulation rejected a common law approach for the following reasons. Although a right to refuse medical treatment exists at common law, the committee believed that very few people are aware of this right. Many patients feel reticent and powerless when it comes to disagreeing with doctors, or refusing treatment. Further, seeking common law remedies is impractical in many instances. The committee considered American case law and noted the difficulty of the common law keeping abreast with medical advances, as well as the widely diverse outcomes of the decided cases.[111]   On the basis of its deliberations, the committee made a number of recommendations, including the enactment of legislation to clarify and protect the common law right to refuse medical treatment.[112] Pursuant to its recommendations, the Medical Treatment Act 1988 was enacted. The Act incorporates a number of recommendations contained in the report of the United States President's Commission for the Study of Ethical Problems in Medicine and Biomedical and Behavioral Research. In addition, it endorses both an autonomy and an ethics of care approach to decision-making.

The Medical Treatment Act 1988

This Act provides that a doctor will be guilty of the offence of medical trespass if he, or she, undertakes or continues treatment after a patient has signed a refusal of treatment certificate. Any doctor, or any person acting under medical instructions, who discontinues treatment in good faith and in reliance on a certificate, is protected from criminal and civil liability. Treatment includes operations, the administration of drugs or other like substances, and any other medical procedure. It does not include palliative care, which is defined as the provision of reasonable medical procedures for relief of pain, suffering and discomfort, and the reasonable provision of food and water. Common law rights of competent patients to refuse medical treatment and practitioners' rights, powers or duties in relation to palliative care, remain unaffected by the Act. A refusal of treatment certificate must be witnessed by a medical practitioner and "another person" who must be satisfied that the patient has clearly and voluntarily expressed an intention to refuse a general, or particular, type of medical treatment. They must also be satisfied that the patient has been informed about his, or her, condition in reasonably sufficient detail to make a decision, and that he, or she, appeared to understand the information. In addition, the patient must be competent and have attained eighteen years of age. Treatment may only be refused for current medical conditions, so that a refusal of treatment certificate cannot be used as an advanced directive. A refusal certificate is not irrevocable and can be changed or modified by a patient. A certificate ceases to be effective once the condition for which it was issued changes.

The Medical Treatment (Enduring Power of Attorney) Act 1990

Amendments to the legislation enable an agent appointed pursuant to an enduring power of attorney, or a guardian of an incompetent patient, to refuse treatment on that patient's behalf. The amendments contain a number of procedural safeguards. These require that a medical practitioner and another person, must be satisfied that an agent, or guardian, has been informed of a patient's current condition, to the same extent as prescribed for competent patients, and that the information has been understood. A surrogate decision-maker may only refuse treatment if it would cause unreasonable distress to the patient or, if there are reasonable grounds for believing that the patient, if competent, after serious consideration of his or her health, would consider the treatment unwarranted. Guardians and agents must complete a prescribed refusal of treatment certificate. In certain circumstances, the Guardianship and Administration Board may suspend or revoke an enduring power of attorney, or a guardianship appointment. In such an event, a certificate of refusal executed by the guardian, or agent, is also revoked. The legislation also provides that any person who, as a beneficiary, improperly procures the execution of a refusal certificate, shall forfeit any entitlement.

Evaluation of the Victorian legislation

An examination of American case law revealed how courts attempt to balance patient autonomy and countervailing State interests when considering treatment refusal issues. The Victorian Medical Treatment Act opts for an unqualified endorsement of patient autonomy. A patient's right to bodily integrity is secured by limiting the activities of others, rather than by requiring the performance of positive acts. Practitioners are not required by the legislation to actively assist a patient in bringing about his or her death. They are however prevented from forcing unwanted treatment on unwilling patients, despite the fact that such treatment may be medically indicated. A difficulty is likely to arise under the legislation where compliance with a certificate requires a positive act which is morally unacceptable to some practitioners, such as turning off a respirator. In these circumstances, it would be appropriate for the practitioner to withdraw, provided another doctor is willing to assume the responsibility. If such an arrangement is not possible, the legislative intent appears to be that a patient's right must prevail over the doctor's ethical or religious views.[113] Such an interpretation is clearly at odds with a beneficence in trust approach and certain theological perspectives which have been previously noted. To minimize the likelihood of such a situation, hospitals and other health care institutions should have a declared policy on termination of treatment, which would enable patients to choose an institution which reflects their own values and beliefs.[114] A right to refuse treatment is not qualified in the legislation by reference to third party rights. It would therefore appear that a patient cannot be forced to undergo treatment in order to provide for the needs of dependents.[115]

The Act seeks to ensure that dying patients receive maximum relief from pain and suffering by providing that palliative care may not be included in a refusal certificate. Because the same procedure, under different circumstances, could be either medical treatment or palliative care, the intention with which a particular procedure is undertaken will be extremely important. The legislative presumption appears to be that palliative care will be provided until it is considered unreasonable. However, it is not clear whether unreasonableness is to be determined from a patient, or a practitioner, perspective. This will be important where patient and doctor do not agree as to the reasonableness of palliative measures. If a situation were to arise under the Victorian legislation, similar to that which occurred in the Bouvia case, a treatment refusal certificate could not be issued to refuse food and water. Consequently, a patient would have to rely on a common law right of refusal basing such a claim in battery.[116] Should the hospital feel that it would be unable to comply with a patient's wishes, it is likely that a judicial resolution would be sought.

An equally important question is whether compliance with a patient's wishes in these circumstances can be deemed aiding and abetting for the purposes of the Criminal law. If suicide is defined as a positive act executed with an intention to end one's life, it is suggested that the issue will not arise in the case of a competent patient who merely refuses treatment, but takes no positive actions, thereby allowing death to occur. Consequently, failure to treat on the part of doctors would not amount to aiding and abetting.[117] This contrasts with the situation in which a doctor believes that suicidal intent underlies patient refusal of ordinary life-sustaining treatment or palliative measures. Some commentators argue that in these circumstances it is unlikely that a doctor would be satisfied of a patient's competence.[118] This interpretation gives rise to the possibility that the right of refusal may in fact be subverted by little more than medical or family disagreement with the direction proposed.[119] Because there can be no absolute right not to be declared incompetent while exercising the right to refuse treatment, this is an area in which reliance must be placed on the integrity of the profession in the exercise of its professional judgement. If a patient becomes suicidal after a refusal certificate has been issued, it is suggested that doctors would be bound by the certificate. It is also contended however, that the onset of the suicidal intent may be regarded as a change in the patient's condition thereby invalidating the certificate.[120] According to another view, a doctor would be able to rely on the provisions of the Victorian Crimes Act to use reasonable force to prevent the commission of suicide. Provided there was clear suicidal intent, it is argued that the relevant provision would justify a doctor refusing to witness a certificate, or treating a patient in contravention of a certificate.[121]

Procedural safeguards have been incorporated in the Act to ensure that a patient's wishes are honoured. A medical practitioner and another person must be satisfied that a patient has freely decided to refuse treatment, that sufficient information has been provided, and that the patient is competent and appeared to understand the information. The Act is silent as to how both parties must satisfy themselves that these criteria have been met. Where one of the parties is not medically qualified, he or she will be heavily dependent upon medical opinion as to competency, and the adequacy of the medical advice on which treatment refusal has been based. If a medical witness has no particular expertise regarding the patient's condition or its treatment, the difficulty of determining the adequacy of information will be compounded.

The legislation has been criticized on the grounds that its emphasis on self-determination may result in patients being abandoned to their autonomy.[122] Once a certificate is signed, there will be little incentive for anyone to intervene, even if they suspect negligent advice has been given, or that the certificate was signed in questionable circumstances. This is because once a certificate is issued, a doctor who undertakes treatment risks being charged with a criminal offence. Moreover, before a certificate's validity may be impugned, it will be necessary to establish bad faith as well as self-interest and incompetence on the part of its witnesses.[123] Reluctance to intervene in the face of a certificate may work to a patient's detriment. In particular, patients who are depressed or otherwise in poor spirits, or who are apprehensive about treatment may, if not otherwise persuaded, refuse treatment which they may subsequently feel pleased to have received. In the absence of legislation like the Victorian Act, it is argued that medical staff would attempt to convince a patient to undertake reasonable treatment. Such action would be motivated by fear of legal liability in the event that a patient in poor spirits suffers, or dies, as a result of negligent advice giving rise to a refusal.[124] Now that the legislation is in place, one critic suggests that the easiest solution for busy doctors faced with difficult, competent, patients, will be to persuade them to sign a refusal certificate.[125] For these reasons, the absence of a provision requiring that patients receive counselling prior to executing a refusal of treatment certificate is viewed as a significant omission.[126]

In the case of incompetent patients, the legislation permits decision-making by a duly appointed surrogate decision-maker who must satisfy a doctor and another person that he or she has understood the information concerning the patient's condition. A surrogate may refuse treatment provided a standard of reasonableness is satisfied. That is to say if he or she believes that treatment would cause unreasonable distress to the patient or, if there are reasonable grounds for believing that the patient, if competent, after serious consideration of his or her health, would consider the treatment unwarranted. It is not clear under the Victorian legislation whether unreasonable distress is limited to physical distress, or whether psychological distress and affronts to dignity may be taken into account. If physical distress is to be the sole criterion, then decision-making of this type is likely to be informed and guided largely by medical opinion.

A decision as to whether an incompetent patient would consider treatment unwarranted is likely to present difficulties under the legislation. This is because substituted judgement is clearly inapplicable in the case of never-competent patients. It is equally inappropriate where a patient has left no indications of his or her intentions, and the surrogate decision-maker is a stranger to the patient. In these situations, ascertaining what the patient would have chosen is a totally speculative exercise. In cases where available evidence is meagre, this test becomes largely an objective one. Where no evidence exists, a purely objective determination will have to be undertaken, at which point the standard becomes indistinguishable from a best interest test. A substituted judgement is more appropriate in the case of once-competent patients. In this situation, when the surrogate undertakes a form of substituted judgement, decision-making will be guided by a surrogate's knowledge of the patient. This form of decision-making accords with the approach of an ethics of care in which a consideration of the particulars of an individual is of fundamental importance. An ethics of care takes into consideration the subjective views of individuals arising out of a particular relationship. The knowledge and insights gleaned from intimate associations are felt to be of particular importance in determining the wishes of incompetent parties. As previously noted, decision-making is subject to a reasonableness criterion under the Victorian Act. This concept is likely to give rise to a broad range of interpretations in the hands of lay individuals. Moreover, it is sufficiently flexible to permit subjective information to be incorporated into decision-making consistent with an ethics of care approach.

OVERVIEW

Death now occurs most frequently in institutional settings involving medical and nursing staff in addition to a patient's family and friends. Contrasting views on treatment refusal issues have been presented above. For some, an unqualified endorsement of patient autonomy is essential, whilst for others, the integrity of the medical profession is inevitably compromised by such an approach. There are those who feel that an insistence on autonomy and rights leads to the abandonment of patients in their time of greatest need. According to an ethics of care approach, an emphasis on rules overshadows the importance of relationships leaving an individual's fate to be determined by objective standards which have nothing to do with the particulars of the individual involved.

The Victorian Medical Treatment Act vests patients (or their duly appointed representatives) with decision-making responsibility. In the case of incompetent patients, the language of the Act permits a degree of discretion to surrogate decision-makers which is consistent with an ethics of care, or responsibility. The Act also seeks to ensure patients will not be abandoned if they refuse treatment by providing that palliative care may not be included in a treatment refusal certificate.

An important aspect of judicial and legislative standards in this area, is that they may serve to encourage people to think about and discuss death, and formally record their preferences. A formal declaration of this nature should become as acceptable as the practice of executing a will, particularly since courts and legislatures are placing great weight on formal communication of patients' wishes.[127]

The Victorian legislation, like judicial determinations, is concerned with decision-making at an individual level. Larry Palmer reminds us however that a consideration of bare legal rights frequently obscures the social and medical context in which choices are made. In addition to ensuring that individuals can exercise a right of refusal there is an urgent need to consider existing institutional constraints on choice. A lack of institutions which offer specialist care, when cure is no longer possible, reduces meaningful choice. Given our rapidly aging population there is need to establish an environment in which elderly, frail and incompetent individuals are cared for and are not regarded as too onerous or too costly to support. For this reason, the Victorian legislation needs to be supplemented by the development of additional institutions in which specialized care is given to those for whom treatment is no longer appropriate.[128] The point is aptly expressed by Robert Burt who has drawn attention to the implications for the elderly as a result of the President's Commission endorsing an individual's right to choose and refuse medical treatment. He cautions as follows:

> There is a considerable social danger lurking in this seemingly self-evident formulation, for the individualistic ideology that lies beneath this formulation, giving it contemporary moral force, also implies that there is no public commitment, no communally acknowledged obligation, to sustain and nurture burdensomely sick people. This implication may only be implicit, it may be glimpsed only as if "through a glass darkly"; but if a gravely ill person, if a sick old person, sees this message embedded in the contemporary social ideology, then he will construe his individualistic "right to die" in a different light. Then he will see this right as something more, as a "duty to die" because no one wants him to act differently, because no one will sustain him in adversity, and because then even he will refuse this caretaking sustenance to himself. [129]

The above assumes a shift in resources away from acute hospital to hospice care. Such a shift will clearly need to be accompanied by a scaling-down of societal and medical expectations concerning medical interventions.[130] Governments cannot guarantee that terminally ill or dying patients are treated with care and compassion. This responsibility falls upon the medical and nursing professions. But governments have an obligation to provide institutions for the humane treatment of those no longer

77

capable of caring for themselves. The provision of hospice care on a broad scale would significantly enhance patient choice in this important area of medical decision-making.

Notes

1. Ramsey P., The Patient as Person. Yale University Press 1970, 116.
2. The circumstances in which incompetent patients may refuse treatment are discussed below. In cases of certain diseases, public health requirements may specify a period of quarantine and\or treatment, with which an individual must comply. Battery is actionable as both a Crime and a Tort, unless it comes within one of the recognized defences of absence of hostility, exigencies of daily life, necessity, or prevention of suicide. For a detailed discussion of these defences see Lanham D., The Right to Chose to Die with Dignity 14 Criminal Law Journal 1990, 401.
3. Inquiry into Options for Dying with Dignity: Final Report of the Social Development Committee, Parliament of Victoria. Victorian Government Printer 1987, 106. (Hereinafter referred to as Report of the Social Development Committee)
4. Id.106-7.
5. Vic.Crimes Act 1958, S.6B, S.463(B).
6. Kennedy I., The Law Relating to the Treatment of the Terminally Ill, in Treat Me Right - Essays in Medical Law and Ethics. Clarendon Press, Oxford 1988, 315, 318-9. The author is heavily indebted to the analysis and ideas contained in this article.
7. Id.323.
8. Where a person acts to end or hasten the end of another's life with the intention or knowledge that this is likely to be the consequence of his or her actions, such a person may be liable for murder, or if death does not result, attempted murder. Crimes Act 1958 (Vic.) S3. as amended by Crimes (Amendment) Act 1986.
9. Bravender Coyle P., An Outline of Certain Legal Issues Relating to the Enquiry, in Report of the Social Development Committee op.cit., Appendix E.
10. Report of the Social Development Committee, op.cit. 128-30. According to some Australian commentators, the argument may be put that once some types of treatment are undertaken, an unlawful killing would be committed if they were withdrawn, even if at a patient's request. Accordingly, a doctor would be regarded as killing the patient, rather than omitting to treat. Where a patient who is being maintained on an artificial life support system, requests that it be turned off, compliance in these circumstances may constitute murder. Dix A. Errington M. Nicholson K. and Powe R., Law For The Medical Profession. Butterworths, 1988, 296.
11. Kennedy op.cit. 322.
12. Findings of poll of 815 Victorians conducted in 1986 by the Morgan Research Centre, indicated that 86.6% of those interviewed were willing to support

passive voluntary euthanasia, while 74% supported active voluntary euthanasia. Report of the Social Development Committee, op.cit. 133-5. For a discussion of this topic in an American context see Callahan D., What Kind of Life - The Limits of Medical Progress. Simon and Schuster Inc. 1990, 224.

13. Charlesworth M., Life, Death, Genes and Ethics: Biotechnology and Bioethics. Australian Broadcasting Corporation 1989, 67. For a challenge to this distinction see Rachels J., The End of Life: Euthanasia and Morality. Oxford University Press 1986. See also Kuhse H., The Sanctity of Life Doctrine in Medicine: A Critique. Oxford University Press 1987. For a summary of the various arguments see Callahan D., What Kind of Life, op.cit. especially Chapter 8.

14. Responses were received from 869 practitioners who were asked whether they ever treated terminally ill or incurable patients of twelve years or over. Those who answered affirmatively were asked if they had ever been asked to hasten death. A series of questions was then posed to 354 doctors who indicated that they had been asked to hasten death. This group were asked the following question: "Have you ever taken active steps to bring about the death of a patient who asked you to do so"? The question was answered by 369 doctors of whom 107 responded that they had taken active measures to bring about the death of a patient who sought their assistance. It appears that despite survey instructions, the number of doctors who answered these questions was as high as 371, indicating that a number of respondents disregarded the instructions. All doctors were asked if they thought it was sometimes right for a doctor to bring about the death of a patient if a patient so requests. A majority of doctors answered in the affirmative. Kuhse H. and Singer P., Doctors' practices and attitudes regarding voluntary euthanasia. 148 Medical Journal of Australia 1988, 623.

15. Submission of the Victorian Medical Board to the Victorian Government Social Development Committee Inquiry into Options for Dying with Dignity. Report of the Social Development Committee op.cit. 132.

16. Id.138-142.

17. S.A. Natural Death Act 1983; N.T. Natural Death Act 1988. In the United States thirty-eight states and the District of Columbia have enacted legislation enabling individuals to make advance directives whereby they can specify the conditions under which they would want treatment terminated. In twelve jurisdictions, legislation includes provisions for incompetent patients who failed to execute a directive when competent. Developments in the Law-Medical Technology and the Law. 103 Harvard Law Review 1990, 1671.

18. Omnibus Budget Reconciliation Act of 1990. Pub.L.No.101-508 ss. 4206, 4751. The legislation is codified in various sections of 42 U.S.C., especially ss. 1395cc, 1396a (West Supp.1991). The legislation is outlined in a subsequent section of this chapter.

19. President's Commission for the Study of Ethical Problems in Biomedical and Behavioral Research. Deciding to Forego Life-Sustaining Treatment Washington D.C, U.S. Government Printing Office 1983,44.

20. Id.44-5, 135.

21. Id.196.

22. Id.46.

23. Id.48.

24. Id.48 -9, 50-1,90, .
25. Deciding to Forego Life-Sustaining Treatment, op.cit. 17.
26. Charlesworth op.cit. 65.
27. Capron A., Legal and Ethical Problems in Decisions for Death. 14 Law Medicine and Health Care 1986, 141.
28. U.S. Congress, Office of Technology Assessment. Life-sustaining technologies and the elderly. OTA-BA-306. U.S. Government Printing Office, 1987, 11, Table 1-1., as cited in Mackay R.D., Terminating life-sustaining treatment - recent US developments. 14 Journal of Medical Ethics 1988, 135, 138.
29. In the Cruzan case, which is discussed below, the United States Supreme Court noted that as a result of medical technology, there has been a burgeoning of cases involving treatment refusal with fifty-four reported decisions between 1976-1988. In Re Cruzan 58 U.S. Law Week 26 June 1990, 4916, 4918.
30. Mackay, op.cit. 138.
31. Capron op.cit. 142.
32. The United States Constitution does not explicitly mention the right of privacy. "Zones of privacy" have been created by constitutional guarantees based on the Bill of Rights and on Constitutional amendments. The United States Supreme Court has created "zones of privacy" in areas including marriage, procreation, contraception, abortion, family relationships and education. United States Congress, Office of Technology Assessment, Unconventional Cancer Treatments, OTA-H-405 (Washington, DC. U.S. Government Printing Office, September 1990), 198, n.2.
33. The Supreme Court has never explicitly held that states are compelled to take this position. Dworkin R., The Right to Death. New York Review of Books, 31 January 1991, 15.
34. In Re Conroy 486 A.2d. 1209.(1985)
35. Id. at 1224. quoting Saikewicz v Superintendent of Belchertown State School (discussed below).
36. Id. at 1226. In Re Farrell, the court stated that courts had consistently agreed that refusal of life-supporting treatment did not constitute an attempt to commit suicide. 529 A.2d.404 (1987) at 411.
37. In Re Farrell supra cit.
38. Brophy v New England Sinai Hospital 497 NE 2d 626 (1986).
39. Bouvia v Superior Court, 179 Cal.App. 3d. 1127, 225 Cal. Rptr. 297 (1986)
40. For a criticism of the way in which courts have interpreted State and professional interest in preserving life see Blake D, State Interests in Terminating Medical Treatment, 19 Hastings Center Report 1989,5.
41. Jacobson v Massachusetts, 197 US 11, 25 S Ct 358,49 L Ed.643 (1905) compulsory smallpox vaccination. Application of President and Directors of Georgetown College Inc.331 F 2d.1000,1008 (DC Cir.) cert.denied, 377 US 978, 84 S Ct.1883, 12 L Ed 2d.746 (1964) ordering mother of a seven month old baby to undergo blood transfusions, despite her religious objections.
42. Raleigh Fitkin-Paul Morgan Memorial Hospital v Anderson 201 A 2d. 537 (1964)
43. This case is discussed in Chapter One.

44. In Re A.C. 573 A2d. 1235, 1990.; Developments in The Law-Medical Technology and the Law 103 Harvard Law Review 1990, 1668.

45. In Re Farrell supra cit.

46. Re Conroy 486 A 2d 1209 (1985) New Jersey Supreme Court.

47. Bouvia v Superior Court, 179 Cal. App. 3d. 1127, 225 Cal.Rptr.297 (1986). For a detailed discussion of this case see Fisher. L., The Suicide Trap: Bouvia v Superior Court and The Right To Refuse Medical Treatment. 21 Loyola of Los Angeles Law Review 1987, 219.

48. The court's discussion of self-determination was brief. 179 Cal.App.3d.at 1137, 225 Cal.Rptr.at 300. In relation to the right of privacy see Id. at 1137; 225 Cal. Rptr. at 301.

49. Id. at 1137; 225 Cal.Rptr. at 300-01

50. Id. at 1135; 225 Cal.Rptr.at 299.

51. Id. at 1143-4; 225 Cal.Rptr.at 305.

52. Id. at 1144; 225 Cal. Rptr. at 305.

53. Id.at 1144; 225 Cal. Rptr. at 306.

54. Id.at 1145; 225 Cal.Rptr.at 306.

55. Id. at 1146; 225 Cal.Rptr.at 307.

56. In re Quinlan, 70 N.J. 10,355 A2d 647, cert.denied, 429 U.S.922(1976)

57. Ibid.

58. In re Conroy, 190 N.J. Super.453,464 A.2d.303 (1983), rev'd,98 N.J.321, 486 A.2d. 1209 (1985)

59. On the basis of these tests the court found that there was insufficient evidence concerning Conroy's beliefs and that the evidence was inconclusive as to whether she was in extreme pain.

60. The court also expressed doubt as to whether a Federal Constitutional right of privacy existed. Cruzan v Harmon, 760 S.W. 2d.408, 417-18 (Mo.1988).

61. Id.419-26.

62. In Re Cruzan 58 U.S. Law Week June 26, 1990, 4916. Rehnquist C.J. delivered the opinion of the Court in which White, Kennedy, O'Connor, and Scalia JJ. joined. O'Connor, J. and Scalia, J. filed concurring opinions. Brennan, J. filed a dissenting opinion in which Marshall and Blackmun JJ. joined. Stevens J. filed a dissenting opinion.

63. Rehnquist C.J., White and Kennedy on the basis of previous cases, assumed, rather than specifically decided, the existence of a right to refuse life-sustaining medical treatment, including artificial hydration and nutrition. Id.4920. O'Connor J. stated that the artificial provision of nutrition and hydration cannot be readily distinguished from other forms of treatment. Further, that "an individual's deeply personal decision to reject medical treatment, including the artificial delivery of food and water", was protected by the Due Process Clause in the Constitution. Id.at 4923. Brennan, Marshall and Blackmun JJ. expressly agreed with this view. Id.at 4927-8. Scalia J. disagreed on the basis that starving oneself to death by the refusal of food and water is no different from taking a positive step to end one's life for the purposes of the common law definition of suicide. Accordingly, the State had a constitutional right to prevent such an action. Id.4925.

64. Id.4921.

65. The New York Times, December 27 1990, 1.
66. Superintendent of Belchertown State School v Saikewicz 373 Mass. 728, 370 N.E.2d.417.
67. Id.742; 370 N.E. 2d. 426.
68. Ibid.
69. Re John Storar 52 N.Y.2d.363,438 N.Y>S>2d.266, 420 N.E.2d 64, cert.denied 454U.S.858, 102 S.Crt.309,70 L.Ed.2d.153, 1981.
70. Powell P.M., Deciding For Others: Rights and Responsibilities in Medical Ethics, M.D.Dissertation, Yale University, 1987. The terms "an ethics of care" and "an ethics of responsibility" are both used as alternatives to an ethics of rights approach which is regarded as characteristic of the dominant moral theories.
71. Id.70-1.
72. Id.72.
73. Id.76-8.
74. Id.73-8.
75. Id.82-7.
76. Id.69.
77. Id.57-9.
78. Id.49-51.
79. Id.92-5.
80. Id.95, 99.
81. Id.99.
82. Id.102.
83. Id.109.
84. Id.111.
85. Id.113.
86. Wolf S., Nancy Beth Cruzan: In No Voice At All. 20 Hastings Center Report 1990, 38,39.
87. Id.39.
88. Id.40.
89. Id.41.
90. Palmer L., Law, Medicine,and Social Justice. Westminster John Knox Press 1989, 8-11.
91. Id.10.
92. Id.93.
93. Id.72-3.
94. Id.73.
95. Id.72.
96. Id.92.
97. Id.94.
98. Id.101.
99. Id.50-1.
100. Pellegrino E. and Thomasma D., For the Patient's Good -The Restoration of Beneficence in Health Care. Oxford University Press 1988, 132, 162.
101. Id.162- 4.
102. Ibid.

103. Id.167-8.
104. Id.202.
105. Id.200-1.
106. Id.191.
107. Id.192.
108. For an evaluation of the legislation see Wolf S., et al. Special Report - Sources of Concern About the Patient Self-Determination Act. 325 New England Journal of Medicine 1991, 1666.
109. In re G.M.Kinney. Unreported judgement, Supreme Court of Victoria, 23 December 1988 (Fullagar J.) In this case Kinney was admitted to hospital in an unconscious state following a drug overdose. An instrument inserted into his throat to aid breathing caused substantial bleeding. The medical staff wished to operate to arrest the bleeding. His wife opposed the operation claiming that her husband wanted to die as he had leukemia and that he had repeatedly told her he did not want intensive care. The wife applied to the Supreme Court for an injunction to prevent the operation. In refusing her application, Mr. Justice Fullagar noted that the Public Advocate, who had been appointed as the patient's guardian, wished the operation to proceed. Moreover, very powerful considerations would be needed to issue an injunction to prevent doctors undertaking life-saving measures. The evidence before the court was insufficient to conclude that the patient wished to die. It was further held that although legislation provides for the signing of a refusal of treatment certificate, no such document had been executed by the appropriate parties in this case.
110. Vic. Medical Treatment Act 1988; Vic. Medical Treatment (Enduring Power of Attorney) Act 1990; S.A. Natural Death Act 1983; N.T. Natural Death Act 1988. The South Australian and Northern Territory legislation permit the execution of advanced directives in relation to refusal of medical treatment.
111. Report of the Social Development Committee, op.cit. 43, 71, 99.
112. Id.142.
113. Lanham op.cit. 428.
114. For a discussion of a need for the development of institutional policies concerning withholding of life-sustaining treatment, see Pollard B., Withdrawing life-sustaining treatment from severely brain-damaged persons. 154 Medical Journal of Australia 1991, 559.
115. An Australian academic suggests that there is a "whiff of slavery" surrounding American decisions in which third party interests have outweighed an individual's right of self-determination and suggests that this limitation should not be accepted in Australia. Lanham op.cit. 401,420.
116. It is suggested that a hospitalized patient could not refuse basic nursing care such as toileting, bathing and linen care on the grounds of hygiene. Kennedy I., The Legal Effect of Requests by the Terminally Ill and Aged not to Receive Further Treatment from Doctors, in Treat Me Right - Essays in Medical Law and Ethics. op.cit. 88, 332.
117. Williams G., "Euthanasia". 41 Medico-Legal Journal 4,31, 1973. For a contrary view which suggests a duty to intervene under the defence of necessity in these circumstances, see Smith J.C. and Hogan B., Criminal Law, 3rd ed. Butterworths 1973, 159.

118. Andrews K., The Medical Treatment Act and the Incompetent Patient. 8 St Vincent's Bioethics Centre Newsletter 1990, 1, 3-4.
119. Dickens B., The right to Natural Death. 26 McGill Law Journal 1981, 847,850-1; Kennedy I., The Legal Effect of Requests by the Terminally Ill and Aged not to Receive Further Treatment from Doctors, in Treat Me Right - Essays in Medical Law and Ethics, op.cit. 336.
120. Andrews op.cit. 3-4.
121. Lanham op.cit. 401,428.
122. Andrews op.cit. 1,3.
123. Clark K., The Medical Treatment Act 1988 - Safeguarding patient's rights or risking patient welfare? Law institute Journal, June 1989, 473,475.
124. Ibid.
125. Ibid.
126. Id.473.
127. The decision in Re Kinney suggests that verbally expressing one's wishes to a relative will not be adequate proof of intention. Recent Federal legislation in the United States aims to encourage people to execute advance directives.
128. As a matter of priority, the Victorian Social Development Committee investigated the provision of palliative and hospice care. It concluded that the provision of both types of care is an essential element in caring for terminally ill patients. Further, it made a number of recommendations in relation to palliative care, including educational measures. Report of the Social Development Committee, op.cit. 221-4.
129. Burt R., The Ideal of Community in the Work of the President's Commission 6 Cardozo Law Review 1984, 267, 284-5.
130. Callahan D., What Kind of Life - The Limits of Medical Progress. Simon and Schuster Inc.1990.

4 Regulation of Human Subject Research

INTRODUCTION

International awareness of the need to protect human research subjects was aroused by revelations of Nazi experimentation upon concentration camp prisoners. The Nuremberg Code, the first international statement on human experimentation, contained several fundamental principles covering biomedical research with human subjects. In 1964, the World Medical Association's draft code of ethics in human experimentation was adopted as the Declaration of Helsinki. A decade later, a revised version of this declaration included a restatement of the reasons justifying the conduct of biomedical research and provided that research protocols should be referred to a specially appointed committee for evaluation and guidance.[1]

The purpose of human subject research is to develop knowledge for the benefit of society, as opposed to treatment of individual patients. Research subjects are invited into a programme, and there is little time or motivation for investigators to become acquainted with, or to be responsive to, the choices and needs of individual participants.[2] Research involves the development of a detailed and relatively inflexible protocol. Formal requirements govern the obtaining of informed consent from participants which is usually obtained during a single meeting. Information is contained in a proposed consent form which must be approved by a specially constituted committee before research commences. In the research enterprise, researchers and subjects are strangers who come together for the purpose of pursuing an investigator's goals. Once research is complete, the relationship is normally terminated.

Research is frequently classified according to whether it is therapeutic or non-therapeutic. Therapeutic research is designed to benefit the participants in addition to a research aim. Experimentation is non-therapeutic when it is undertaken solely to obtain information for the benefit of others without the intention of treating the particular research subjects. Both the United States National Commission for the Protection of Human Subjects of Biomedical and Behavioral Research and the Canadian Medical Research Council have rejected this distinction on the grounds that it is illogical, and because it may give rise to harmful misconceptions. According to the Canadian Medical Research Council, because the dichotomy implies that therapeutic research will directly benefit a subject, "the need for full and careful consent, considered to be so important in non-therapeutic research, is often glossed over because therapeutic research is confounded with treatment or care".[3]   Robert Levine suggests that in the United States, concern is not focused on whether a research project is therapeutic or not, but on whether particular procedures "hold out the prospect of direct benefit for the individual subject, or ... [are] likely to contribute to the subject's well-being...".[4]

Controlled trials are a common feature of medical experimentation. To determine whether a new drug is more effective than an existing one, or no treatment at all, it is administered to a group of patients or healthy volunteers, and simultaneously withheld from a similar group. The control group does not receive the therapy under consideration. It may however receive a different dose of the drug under investigation, another therapy, a placebo, or no therapy at all. To ensure objectivity, the "double-blind" technique and randomization are commonly employed. According to the former technique, neither researchers nor research participants are aware of the classification of the group to which they have been assigned. In a randomized clinical trial (RCT), patients are assigned to treatment categories by a randomizing method which it is believed will eliminate any researcher bias or any unsuspected interfering factor.[5] The RTC has been described as the "gold standard" by which experimental treatments are judged to be useful, worthless or dangerous.[6] The quality of the data obtained in this manner is felt to provide doctors and patients with the opportunity to make informed decisions.[7] Some critics argue however, that in the case of a universally fatal disease such as AIDS, the use of historical or literature controls is more appropriate.[8]

HUMAN SUBJECT RESEARCH POLICY AND REGULATION IN THE UNITED STATES

Historical background

The history of human subject research in the United States reveals fundamental changes in societal attitudes and government policies about the desirability of unfettered scientific autonomy. During the post World War Two period, medical research developed with minimum government intervention. There was widespread public confidence in the integrity of scientific investigators as a result of medical achievements, including the conquest of infectious diseases through immunization and new drugs. Within the medical community there was a general scepticism about a need for ethical guidelines or codes. At common law, the few decided cases involving clinical practice endorsed professional autonomy by the application of a reasonable doctor (or professional practice) standard of care. Judicial deference to medical opinion re-enforced notions of scientific autonomy prevalent in the biomedical community, which, in this respect, made no distinction between clinicians and researchers.[9] During the sixties and seventies, social and political philosophy and theory emphasising self-determination and individual rights, combined with anti-authoritarian and sectarian sentiments. The general mood of the times favoured challenging a medical model in which investigators' beneficence and integrity was accepted as a substitute for patient consent. It was equally disposed to challenging a research ethic based on social utility.[10]

A number of factors appear to have prompted Federal government intervention in human subject research. Increased government funding heightened interest in monitoring research expenditures during the post World War Two period.[11] Publicity surrounding unethical experimentation shaped public attitudes, and served as a catalyst for increased government intervention. An article published in 1966 by American physician, Henry Beecher, documented some twenty-two human subject experiments, drawn from a much wider sample, which he claimed were ethically unacceptable.[12] Several of these involved exposing vulnerable and disadvantaged subjects to what he regarded as an unacceptable ratio of risk to benefit. In one such case, chloramphenicol, a drug with known fatal side-effects, was administered to patients without their knowledge. Another case involved experimentation on mentally disabled children at the Willowbrook State School in New York.[13] On the basis of these findings, he concluded that unethical or ethically questionable procedures were not uncommon, and that there was widespread disregard of subjects' rights by researchers. In keeping with contemporary professional attitudes, Beecher suggested that the best protection against such abuses was the conscience of the responsible investigator.[14]

Subsequent publicity about flagrant research abuses included experiments at the Jewish Chronic Diseases Hospital, which were partly funded by the Public Health Service (PHS). In these experiments, elderly and in some cases, senile patients with various chronic debilitating diseases were injected with live cancer cells. The purpose of this study was to determine whether patient rejection of these cells was caused by their cancer or by debilitation. Patients were not informed of the cancerous nature of the cells because previous studies indicated that there was no foreseeable danger to the individuals involved, and because it was believed that such information might agitate them unnecessarily. The matter eventually came to the attention of the hospital's Board of Directors. It was subsequently raised before a hearing panel of the New York State Board of Regents which ruled that the doctors involved had erred in not obtaining the informed consent of their subjects. The decision also indicated that informed consent is always necessary to protect individual self-determination, even if the risks involved are minimal and the potential benefits significant.[15]

Experiments at Willowbrook State Hospital involved deliberately injecting mentally handicapped children with viral hepatitis as part of a study designed to develop an effective prophylactic against this disease. Although parents of the children consented to oral administration or injection of the virus, they were not apprised of the appreciable risks involved. The consent forms used in the study gave the impression that the children were to receive a vaccine against the virus. When overcrowding halted the admission of new patients, those children whose parents volunteered them for the study were admitted. This action gave rise to the subsequent suggestion that parents had been coerced into volunteering their children.[16]

One of the most disturbing examples of unethical experimentation was initiated at the Tuskegee Institute in Alabama in 1932. The study involved the observation of untreated syphilis in four hundred black males.[17] The subjects were unaware that they were involved in a non-therapeutic experiment. Moreover, in the early fifties, when penicillin became widely available as the preferred treatment, they were not advised about or given access to the drug. In response to questions raised by a social worker in 1966, and again in 1968, a panel was established by the PHS to examine ethical issues of the experiment. Continued withholding of treatment from participants was included in its recommendations. Despite reports of this experiment in the medical literature, it was not until 1972, following national press coverage, that the Department of Health Education and Welfare (DHEW) finally halted the study. At that time, seventy-four of the subjects were still alive, at least twenty-eight having died as a result of syphilis.

An ad hoc advisory panel was established by DHEW to review the study together with existing human subject research policies. The panel recommended that risk-benefit analysis should no longer be solely determined by the scientific community and that a permanent body should be established to regulate Federally funded research. Subsequent Congressional hearings involved the Tuskagee experiment and other controversial areas of research. These hearings, as well as the findings of various studies commissioned by the Federal Food and Drug Administration (FDA) and the PHS, revealed the inadequacy of government policies and controls. As a result of publicity about unethical experimentation, public and government attitudes changed so that researchers were no longer presumed to always act in their subjects' best interests.[18] This in turn prompted a variety of measures designed to limit professional autonomy, including the establishment of the National Commission for the Protection of Human Subjects of Biomedical and Behavioral Research and the Institutional Review Board (IRB) system.[19] In the following sections, the role of the FDA and the National Institutes of Health (NIH) in the regulation of human subject research is outlined. Each of these organizations forms part of the PHS, although this was not so in the case of the FDA prior to 1968. The NIH is involved in supporting and conducting biomedical and behaviourial research.[20] In contrast, the FDA is a regulatory body vested with a broad responsibility which includes new drug evaluation and approval, and the regulation of prescription drug promotional practices.

The Federal Food and Drug Administration (FDA)

FDA regulatory responsibility includes granting marketing approval for prescription drugs. These products include any chemical or biological substances which affect the structure or any function of the body and which are intended for use in the diagnosis, cure, mitigation, treatment or prevention of disease.[21]

Investigational new drugs

To obtain marketing approval for its product, a sponsor, usually the manufacturer, must submit evidence of a drug's safety and effectiveness, based on animal and in vitro studies, as well as reports of clinical investigations involving human subjects.[22] Prior to commencing human investigations, an Investigational New Drug application (IND) must be submitted to the FDA.[23] An IND application contains information about a drug's chemistry, pharmacology, toxicology and manufacturing. Animal studies data must establish that the drug is safe for use in humans.[24] If the application contains sufficient information to meet FDA requirements, an IND is allowed to proceed, exempting a sponsor from the prohibition on interstate shipping of unapproved drugs. Only the sponsor and those investigators specifically listed in an IND are permitted to study the drug.[25] The IND requirements, which apply during the time a drug is under active investigation, serve as a monitoring device which enables the FDA to ensure the proper conduct of clinical trials.[26]

The drug development process involving human subjects has three phases which are defined in FDA regulations.[27] Although subject to variations, generally speaking Phase 1 which usually takes a year, includes clinical pharmacology testing in between 10 to 50 healthy subjects. Studies for drugs for conditions such as AIDS or cancer, or of a highly toxic drug, may involve patients with the target disease. During short-term tolerance and clinical pharmacology studies, investigators study the manner in which the drug is tolerated, metabolized and excreted. In addition, they begin to study the drug's safety, together with dosage levels and routes of administration. Phase 2, which normally takes two years or more, involves from 50 to 200 subjects and is concerned with gathering additional safety information and determining whether there is evidence of efficacy. Phase 3, which is undertaken over approximately three years, may include from one to several thousand patients and is designed to expand on the safety and efficacy data obtained in earlier stages.[28] At the end of this phase, there should be information establishing effectiveness for specific indications for use, as well as concerning those groups at special risk. Review focuses on different considerations at each stage of the clinical investigation. In reviewing Phase 1 submissions, the FDA is concerned with participants' rights and ensuring that subjects are not exposed to unreasonable risks. Phase 2 and 3 submissions are assessed to determine whether they are designed to yield data capable of meeting FDA requirements for pre-marketing approval.[29]

New drug approval

To obtain FDA marketing approval for a product, sponsors are required on completion of clinical testing to submit a new drug application (NDA) outlining results of the concluded studies. In 1962, the Federal Food Drug and Cosmetic Act was amended largely in response to the thalidomide disaster. Amongst other things, the amendments imposed stricter controls on the clinical testing of new drugs. Researchers were now required to inform subjects that a drug was being used for investigational purposes and to obtain their consent, except where this was not feasible or deemed not to be in the subjects' best interests.[30] The amendments also required that a drug could not be marketed until "substantial evidence" of efficacy and safety for its intended conditions of use had been provided. The justification for these stringent statutory requirements is that, unlike IND review which is concerned with approval for testing in relatively small numbers of subjects, NDA review is premised on the fact that once approved, a drug will be used by a much larger patient population.[31]

The decision to approve a drug for marketing involves a risk-benefit analysis in which therapeutic benefits are weighed against potential risks. Generally speaking, if the benefits associated with the use of a particular drug outweigh the possible risks of injury or death, a drug will be approved. Risk-benefit analysis may be expected to vary according to the circumstances so that a drug designed for the treatment of minor ailments will be subject to different safety and effectiveness evaluations from those which are applied to drugs designed for life-threatening diseases. In evaluating a new drug, no independent testing is undertaken by the FDA. If a manufacturer fails to satisfy the standard of proof in relation to safety and efficacy, approval may be withheld until further tests are conducted. Ultimately, the agency must rely on data submitted to it by manufacturers. Although drug manufacturers are required to disclose information concerning adverse effects, on occasion, data have been found to be culpably incomplete.[32]

Due to the limited nature of information generated by pre-marketing studies, a decision to grant marketing approval is necessarily made with the knowledge that a drug will be available to consumers before all its hazards are fully recognized. Pre-marketing studies information is incomplete for a variety of reasons. First, because clinical studies involve a limited number of patients, rare reactions, even though serious, are seldom detected. Second, due to the limited duration of these studies, long term effects frequently cannot be determined. Third, variables found in everyday treatment situations are excluded from clinical studies. Fourth, it is customary to exclude patients with illnesses which are different from the indication for therapy of the drug being studied, yet these illnesses may affect either efficacy or toxicity.[33] Marketing approval includes an evaluation of labelling and promotional materials associated with prescription drugs. Detailed regulation of the form and content of these materials seeks to ensure rational prescribing by requiring, amongst other things, that practitioners are notified of the conditions under which they can safely prescribe a particular drug. A medical practitioner may prescribe a drug for purposes other than its approved conditions without obtaining FDA approval. Such a course of action could constitute both a breach of common law and professional standards. The average time between submission of an NDA and FDA approval is approximately three years. Once approved, post-marketing surveillance may lead to a drug being removed from the market.

Institutional review boards

Since 1971, all research proposals are required to be reviewed by an institutional review board (IRB). Requirements about composition and functions of these bodies which include evaluation, approval and monitoring of human subject research activities are contained in FDA regulations.[34] The purpose of IRB review is to ensure a reasonable risk-benefit ratio, the equitable selection of research subjects, compliance with informed consent provisions, and that adequate monitoring activities will be undertaken. A common regulatory framework has been established for IRBs reviewing research conducted or funded by either the Department of Health and Human Services (DHHS) or the FDA.[35]

National Institutes of Health (NIH)

Until 1937, the bulk of medical research financed by the Federal government was conducted in government laboratories. In that year, a National Cancer Institute was established under the umbrella of NIH, together with a system of PHS grants for extramural research. During the forties, funding for medical research increased dramatically. The PHS assumed a dominant role in medical research with responsibility for the administration of public health grants and its own intramural research at NIH. In 1944 it was authorized to award grants for outside investigations in research other than cancer.[36] Nevertheless, its control over the conduct of funded research programmes was confined to a power to refuse awarding a research grant. During this period, the PHS attitude toward unregulated research appears to have been based on trust in professional standards and the integrity of investigators. It was not until 1953 that the first Federal policy statement was issued requiring peer review of human subject research conducted at the newly established NIH Clinical Centre.[37] Largely due to uncritical professional and public attitudes towards the research establishment, this policy was not implemented during the following decade by any other research institutions.[38] In 1964, a group headed by an NIH official was charged with defining government's ethical and legal obligations concerning research review. The group recommended that moral and ethical principles should be formulated by a professional group. James Shannon, Director of NIH, did not agree. Instead, Shannon believed that research principles would be more appropriately formulated by a body which incorporated broader social interests. It was this insight which foreshadowed the development of lay participation in experimentation review.[39]

The 1966 PHS guidelines

In 1966, research guidelines were issued by the Surgeon General of the PHS against a background of publicity about ethically dubious experimentation. The implementation of voluntary guidelines was partly due to an NIH attitude that it would not be possible to design a legal code which would be appropriate in all circumstances. An equally important factor was the perception that the imposition of legal standards and sanctions would not be acceptable to the medical community.[40] The requirement of prior committee review was subsequently extended to all research subject to PHS approval.[41] Its purpose was to ensure an independent evaluation of subjects' rights and welfare, the appropriateness of methods of obtaining informed consent and of

91

risk-benefit evaluation. Whilst government policy acknowledged the need to scrutinize research, the system which was established was one of institutional peer review. As a result, review procedures remained subject to professional control.[42] Despite the inclusion of informed consent requirements in the voluntary guidelines, greater emphasis appears to have been placed on the review process. This may well have been due to general scepticism about informed consent amongst researchers and NIH personnel.[43] Such an attitude is not surprising, given that at this time courts were only beginning to develop legal doctrine governing information disclosure. David Rothman argues that the guidelines were not entirely innovative since their purpose was to protect subjects, rather than to maximize their autonomy and free choice. Further, he maintains that the guidelines reflected the persistence of the presumption that researchers, rather than subjects, are best placed to ensure subjects' well-being.[44] As will be explained, additional events were necessary to overturn this presumption.

PHS and DHEW policy initiatives 1969-71

Following publication of Beecher's article in 1966, and revelations of NIH research abuses, government policy began to reflect changing attitudes towards research autonomy and lay participation in review bodies. PHS guidelines issued in 1969 stated that a review committee composed exclusively of biomedical scientists would be inadequate and that a committee "must be composed of sufficient members with varying backgrounds to assure complete and adequate review..".[45] Committee members with competencies in addition to scientific expertise were required to assess research taking into account institutional regulations, relevant law, professional standards, and community acceptance.[46] The guidelines also stipulated that research subjects must receive a fair explanation of research procedures and objectives, together with a statement of possible benefits, hazards and discomforts. Although designed to provide broad standards which could be applied at the discretion of individual committees, the guidelines gave rise to confusion and dissatisfaction ultimately leading to a demand for more precise standards.

In 1971, DHEW published the Institutional Guide to DHEW Policy on the Protection of Human Subjects which was applicable to all its programmes and activities.[47] Informed consent was defined as including a fair explanation of research procedures, a description of risks, benefits, discomforts and alternative procedures, together with a statement advising that a subject is free to withdraw at any time. Procedures were specified for obtaining informed consent. Consent could be either oral or written, and could be obtained following participation in research provided a complete and prompt debriefing was given. In some circumstances, it could be inferred from voluntary participation in adequately advertised research activities.[48] These additional requirements considerably weakened consent regulation. Committee composition, research subject recruitment and methods for assessing the adequacy of informed consent were identified, one year later, as continuing problems by the Director of NIH. Subsequently these issues were examined in Congressional hearings together with evidence about the Willowbrook and Tuskagee experiments.[49] As a result, formal regulations governing human subject research replaced DHEW guidelines. In addition, the National Research Act 1974 was enacted which established the National Commission for the Protection of Human Subjects of Biomedical and Behavioral Research.

The 1974 Federal regulations

In 1974, Federal regulations were enacted which reflected a commitment to informed consent and independent review. These regulations required review committees to include "persons whose primary concerns lie in these areas of legal, professional, and community acceptability rather than in the conduct of research, development, and service programmes of the type supported by DHEW".[50] Although the definition of informed consent was substantially the same as that contained in the 1971 guide, written consent was required, except where subjects were exposed to minimum risks, and obtaining consent could be dispensed with only in strictly limited circumstances.[51] Faden and Beauchamp contend that the 1974 regulations contained only minor revisions of the 1971 DHEW guidelines. Despite the "rapidly rising tide of concern about respect for subjects' rights of autonomous choice", they suggest that risk reduction remained the main focus of committee review.[52] As will be explained in the following section, the concept of patients' autonomy was one of the concerns of a National Commission with special responsibilities in the area of human subject research.

The National Commission for the Protection of Human Subjects of Biomedical and Behavioral Research 1974-8

During the four years of its existence, the National Commission was concerned with policy formulation and identifying and evaluating assumptions underlying research practices. It was also responsible for reviewing problems and practices associated with protecting research subjects' rights and welfare, including procedures for obtaining informed consent, and examining the Institutional Review Board system.[53] Membership included lawyers, doctors, ethicists, theologians, scientists, health administrators and government personnel.[54] Although inter-disciplinary in nature, the Commission was not truly representative in the absence of lay members.

Ethical principles governing research

Respect for persons, beneficence and justice were identified by the Commission as appropriate ethical principles for governing human subject research.

Respect for persons

According to the Commission, respect for persons requires that individuals are treated as autonomous agents who are capable of deliberation about personal goals, and of acting in accordance with such direction.[55] Research subjects must be adequately informed so that they can freely decide, in accordance with their own values, whether or not to participate in experimentation.[56] The Commission considered that, in the absence of compelling reasons, it would be disrespectful of autonomy to repudiate an individual's considered judgement, or to prevent action on the basis of such judgement.[57] In relation to non-beneficial procedures, the Commission commented as follows:

> ....if the prospective subjects are normal adults, the primary responsibility
> of the IRB should be to assure that sufficient information will be disclosed
> .... provided the research does not present an extreme case of
> unreasonable risks.[58]

In contrast to previous government policies which interpreted the purpose of informed consent provisions in terms of securing subjects' well being, the Commission linked the purpose of informed consent with protection of autonomy and personal dignity.[59] Its adoption of a reasonable person standard of information disclosure, in preference to a professionally-based standard, accorded with the emphasis placed on patient autonomy and self-determination in contemporaneous literature and debate. At the same time, American courts were abandoning a professionally determined disclosure standard in a clinical context, in preference for a rule based on the information needs of the reasonable patient. The high water mark of this approach was reached in 1972 in the case Canterbury v Spence. Although many jurisdictions subsequently reverted to a professionally based standard for clinical relationships, the reasonable person standard continues to govern research practices in the United States.[60]

Beneficence and justice

The Commission interpreted beneficence as creating obligations to secure subjects' well being, including the discovery of information which contributes to this goal for society's future good.[61] A utilitarian concept of justice was rejected on the grounds that it did not accord with prevailing notions of equality, and because it failed to take sufficient account of individual weaknesses and vulnerabilities. The Commission's definition of justice is incorporated in its statement on research selection procedures which requires scrutiny of selection processes to prevent systematic selection of vulnerable groups. It further stated that the benefits of research should not be available solely on the basis of ability to pay.[62] Certain assumptions were prevalent in scientific and lay communities at the time of the Commission's deliberations. These were first, that research is justified by the benefits which it confers upon society. Second, that the benevolence and trustworthiness of researchers justifies professional responsibility for decision-making. Third, that research is not a political matter and should be self-regulating. The research principles identified by the Commission challenged these assumptions. Because of this challenge and the atmosphere created by Congressional hearings, it is suggested that research is now conducted in an atmosphere quite different from that of the past.[63]

The 1981 regulations and subsequent amendments

The politicizing of research resulted in the enactment of DHHS regulations which endorsed the ethical principles identified by the Commission.[64]   The regulations carefully balance these principles so that beneficence is tempered by respect for persons. Translated into everyday practice, this means that researchers should only conduct experiments which minimize possible harm to participants. Where risks can be reduced, a subject's willingness to participate does not relieve researchers of the obligation to reduce such risks.[65] A balance is also sought in risk-benefit evaluation by providing that any "risks to the subject (must be) reasonable in relation to anticipated benefits, if any, and the importance of the knowledge that may reasonably be expected to result".[66] Investigators' discretion is subject to informed consent requirements and a system of independent IRB review.[67]

Informed consent

In obtaining written consent, investigators must clearly indicate the research nature of the proposed activity, its purpose, and the procedures involved. Participants must be advised of any reasonably foreseeable risks or discomforts, any expected benefits, and of their right to withdraw at any time without penalty or loss of any benefits to which they are entitled. Alternative procedures, or treatment, must be disclosed. An assurance must be given that participants will be notified of any significant new findings which could affect their willingness to participate. Information is to be provided concerning the availability of medical treatment should injury occur, and where further information may be obtained. Consent should not be obtained unless participants have had an adequate opportunity to consider whether or not to participate.[68]   Subjects must be informed, where indicated, that unforeseeable risks may be involved and that participation may be terminated by the investigator, without regard to their consent. Subsequent amendments provide that consent must not include any waiver of legal rights.[69]   In addition to these regulatory requirements, IRBs must also determine whether consent forms should inform participants of randomization.[70]

IRB review

Regulations require that IRB membership reflects a diversity in terms of professional training, cultural backgrounds, gender and race. At least one member with non-scientific interests should be included, as well as one who is not associated with the research institution. Where an IRB is regularly involved in reviewing vulnerable research populations, at least one member must be responsible for subjects' welfare.[71] Although an IRB may suggest changes to a research protocol, it cannot compel investigators to comply. The ultimate sanctioning power of these bodies is the withholding of approval of a protocol.[72] IRBs are authorized to monitor research activities to determine whether the relevant standards are being observed. In cases of non-compliance or unanticipated serious harm to subjects, an IRB may suspend or terminate research. Serious or continuing non-compliance by investigators must be reported by an IRB both to the institution concerned and to the Federal government.[73] Although the DHHS regulations only apply to Federally funded projects, they have been adopted by almost all institutions regardless of funding source. In addition, some States have enacted research regulations modelled on Federal standards.[74] Government policies and legislative standards have reportedly had "a revolutionary impact" on human subject research activities in the United States.[75] This, in turn, has contributed to a gradual restoration of public confidence in human subject research.[76]

AUSTRALIAN REGULATION OF HUMAN SUBJECT RESEARCH

NHMRC policy and recommendations concerning human subject research

The National Health and Medical Research Council (NHMRC), established in 1936 by an order of the Commonwealth Governor-General, plays a key role in the regulation of human subject research in Australia. Its functions include making recommendations to Commonwealth and State governments on matters of medical research, and to the Commonwealth in relation to medical research expenditure. In 1966, the NHMRC issued a statement based on the Declaration of Helsinki which contained general research guidelines, but which did not specify a need for institutional peer review. A decade later, in response to proposed amendments to the Declaration of Helsinki establishing committee review and the establishment of IRBs in the United States, the NHMRC recommended the establishment of research committees to assess NHMRC grant applications. Because a system of peer review was envisaged, the only stipulation concerning committee composition was that membership should include at least one individual unconnected with the institution.[77]

It was not until 1982 that NHMRC guidelines required membership of review committees to include a range of non-scientific interests and to reflect age and gender differences. It was specifically required that a person unconnected with the research institution, a minister of religion, a lawyer, a medical graduate with research experience and a lay man and woman be included. The guidelines provided that one individual could act in more than one of these capacities.[78] The following year, the NHMRC established the Medical Research Ethics Committee (MREC) to review ethical research principles and to oversee the Institutional Ethics Committee (IEC) system.[79] This committee was disbanded in 1991 together with the National Bioethics Consultative Committee. The functions of these two bodies is combined in the recently established Health Ethics Advisory committee, which operates within the framework of the NHMRC. A subsequent revision of the guidelines recommended making compliance with IEC composition and functioning requirements mandatory.[80] As a result, only institutions which conform with these conditions are eligible to receive NHMRC funding for research.[81] The system is limited in so far as NHMRC powers of approval do not extend to research funded by other grant-giving bodies, or private research. In fact, the NHMRC research fund provides little more than one quarter of the total funds spent annually in medical research in Australia.[82] In 1985, as a result of further revision to IEC compositional provisions, the stipulation that one person could represent the interests in more than one category was omitted.[83]

Currently, the functions of IECs include consideration of the ethical implications and acceptability of all proposed research protocols, monitoring approved projects and maintaining an approved projects register.[84] In carrying out these functions, IECs are required to be guided by the Declaration of Helsinki 1975 and to take account of local, cultural and social attitudes in decision-making. Committees must ensure that participants' written consent has been obtained and that comprehensible information has been provided about the purpose, methods, demands, risks, inconveniences and discomforts of the study. In addition, committees are responsible for ensuring that the rights of individual patients or research participants take precedence over the expected benefits to human knowledge in the community.[85]

Evaluation of Australian review practices

A number of shortcomings in IEC review procedures were identified in a recent study.[86] Findings in relation to committee composition requirements indicated a seventy-five per cent compliance rate with NHMRC guidelines. The average committee comprises four medical graduates, (including administrators, clinicians and researchers), two lay members, a lawyer, a Minister of Religion and representatives of two or three other professions. Only twenty-seven per cent of respondents indicated the inclusion of an individual who could be regarded as representing patient interests, and nineteen per cent reported a member who could be regarded as a community interest group representative.[87] Responses also revealed the appointment of lay members largely on the basis of recommendations from within the relevant committee or institution. This raises concerns that the NHMRC requirement for lay members to be independent of an institution is not being observed.[88] Findings about convening meetings in the absence of particular members suggests a variation in the importance attached to individual members. The attendance of medical graduates is regarded as most necessary, followed by medical researchers and lay members, whilst the presence of lawyers and Ministers of Religion is not perceived as crucial. In order to preserve the representative nature of IECs, it has been recommended that a policy for a minimum quorum be developed which would require the presence of at least two non-institutional members.[89] The impartiality of some decisions was questioned in responses which indicated that some committee members remain during the consideration of their own project.[90] Although the NHMRC guidelines stipulate that IECs monitor research until its completion, survey responses indicate that the committees have not implemented consistent surveillance methods. For this reason, it has been suggested that committees should adopt a more active monitoring role.[91] Despite these shortcomings, the authors of the survey nevertheless conclude that Australian research institutions have been responsive to the NHMRC guidelines, and that the NHMRC has been successful in according greater importance to ethical review of human subject research in Australia.[92]

Therapeutic Goods Administration (TGA) research guidelines 1991

Recent TGA guidelines governing clinical research practices include detailed provisions concerning informed consent.[93]   The required information closely resembles that specified in the 1981 American regulations outlined above.[94] The guidelines additionally require that subjects be advised of randomization procedures, the use of placebo where relevant and, in language reminiscent of Jay Katz, of the uncertainties of the experiment. The guidelines also focus on the process of obtaining informed consent. The specified information, both oral and written, must be provided in comprehensible language and subjects must receive a copy of the consent form. Information should be provided by an investigator, or qualified delegate, to ensure that an ethical involvement with subjects is maintained. Subjects must be given sufficient time to consider the information and the individual obtaining consent should make an effort to be fully satisfied that the subject understands the nature of the investigation.[95]

THEORIES AND VIEWS ON INFORMED CONSENT

As described above, American and Australian government policy was implemented to protect research subjects from unethical experimentation. The concept of informed consent and independent scrutiny of research were incorporated into regulatory policies and regulations as necessary counter-measures to safeguard the interests of research subjects. But whilst safety remained a major concern of governments and citizens, other concepts, including autonomy, began to be applied in a research context. In the United States, a national commission identified ethical principles relevant to human subject research. These principles were subsequently incorporated into DHHS regulations. NHMRC and TGA voluntary guidelines were implemented in Australia. The TGA guidelines, like the American regulations, reflect ideas and theoretical perspectives about human subject research regulatory policy which have informed public debate in recent times. In the following sections, some perspectives concerning informed consent and ethics committee review which have helped to shape human subject research regulatory policy are outlined.

Legal perspectives

The role of Australian and American common law in shaping information disclosure was outlined in Chapter Two. The common law has not assumed the same significant role in regulating informed consent in human subject research. The dearth of litigated cases involving informed consent in a research context in the United States may well be due to the salutary effect of the regulations. The reasonable person standard of information disclosure governs research practices in the United States. In Canterbury v Spence, this standard was applied in a clinical context. Stressing the importance of patient self-determination, the court rejected the reasonable doctor standard according to which the adequacy of information disclosure is determined with reference to prevailing medical practice. Instead, it was held that a risk should be disclosed when "a reasonable person, in what the physician knows or should know to be the patient's position, would be likely to attach significance to risks or cluster of risks in deciding whether or not to forego the proposed therapy".[96]   As previously explained, post-Canterbury, courts in many American jurisdictions reverted to a reasonable doctor standard for determining the adequacy of disclosure in the clinical relationship.

In the Canadian case Halushka v University of Saskatchewan, the plaintiff, who was a university student, agreed for the sum of fifty dollars, to be involved in a trial of a new anaesthetic at the University hospital.[97] Although the defendants had not previously used or tested the anaesthetic, they nevertheless reassured the plaintiff that it would be a safe test. Following a description of the procedures by one of the defendants, the plaintiff signed a consent form. The experimental procedure conformed with what had been described to the plaintiff, except that a catheter was inserted into a vein in his arm and advanced through the various heart chambers and positioned in the pulmonary artery. During the test, the plaintiff suffered a complete cardiac arrest and was unconscious for four days. As a result, it was decided that the anaesthetic was unsafe and it was subsequently withdrawn from use in the University hospital. In finding for the plaintiff, the court held that the duty owed by a researcher to a subject is at least as great, if not greater than, the duty owed by a doctor to a patient. The court noted that, unlike clinical practice, there can be no exceptions to the obligation to disclose, and that research participants are entitled to a full and frank disclosure of all the facts, probabilities and opinions which a reasonable person might be expected to consider before consenting to participate. The research subject's right of self-determination and interest in choice were clearly factors which influenced the judgement. Observing that the plaintiff had not been advised that the catheter would enter his heart, the court was of the opinion that although this did not cause the cardiac arrest, it was a circumstance which, if it had been drawn to the plaintiff's attention, might well have influenced him to withhold consent and as such, it should have been disclosed.

The right of research subjects to a full and frank disclosure has been recently recognized by a New Zealand Judge. In the course of an enquiry concerning the unethical treatment of women patients at a major Auckland hospital, Judge Cartwright commented as follows:

> the patient is entitled to all relevant information concerning her treatment, the options for treatment, and all information concerning her possible inclusion in a research trial. The focus should be centered on the patient, and not on the doctor. It is a principle designed to protect and preserve the patient's rights, not to protect the doctor from liability.[98]

Whether the fact of randomization should be disclosed to research subjects is a widely debated issue. Arguments against disclosure suggest that where alternative treatments are not known to produce significantly different results, doctors would have to make an arbitrary choice so that informing patients of assignment by computer does not provide additional protection and is unnecessary.[99] Charles Fried argues that where the choice between the two treatments is not in equipoise, failure to disclose the fact of randomization is deceptive.[100] This is so, Fried claims, because non-disclosure fails to notify the patient that his or her interests are being sacrificed for the sake of experimental design. Such a sacrifice may take the form of exposing the patient to the risk of a less favoured treatment. It can also occur by failing to make adequate inquiries about a patient's particular circumstances and values in order to determine whether the condition of equipoise exists in this particular case.[101] Even where alternative treatments are really in equipoise for a particular patient, failure to disclose randomization deprives patients of information which many would consider relevant. Disclosure is of the utmost importance, because patients have an interest in knowing about and participating in processes that affect their most vital interests.[102]

Medical perspectives

A variety of medical attitudes exists about human subject research regulation. Some doctors believe that regulation in this area is both impractical and unnecessary. Others argue that it is necessary to protect subjects and to educate researchers. The practical value of consent requirements has been challenged on the ground that attempts to protect a subject's interest, independent of an investigator, are futile because of the degree of control and influence exerted by researchers.[103] In a seminal article, **Informed (but uneducated) Consent**, the late Franz Ingelfinger argued that an element of coercion is always involved in research.[104] This is particularly so in the case of a hospitalized patient who can scarcely be regarded as exercising free choice when agreeing to join the research programme of the person on whom all hope is anchored. According to Ingelfinger, obtaining an informed consent is an impossibility because patients are not capable of understanding the information provided and consequently are unable to assess the risks and benefits involved. For Ingelfinger, an investigator and a subject could not become involved in some common cause or participate in the research enterprise as joint adventurers because he believed that a subject's consent "is marked by neither adequate understanding nor total freedom of choice". [105] To achieve a mutual undertaking of this nature, he suggested that an educated and comprehending consent would be necessary. Despite detailed regulations, Ingelfinger characterized the process of obtaining an informed consent as an elaborate ritual which, in the case of uneducated and uncomprehending subjects, confers no more than the "semblance of propriety" on experimentation. He concluded that in these circumstances, the only real protection for the subject is the "conscience and compassion of the investigator".[106]

Certain medical views suggest that it is inappropriate to obtain written consent from patients suffering from acute illnesses. Because acutely ill patients are often confused by either over-simplified or detailed descriptions of intended research, the obtaining of consent has been described as a "self-deluding exercise designed only to re-assure ethics committees (and investigators) that they are discharging their moral obligations".[107] According to another view, written consent requirements should be dispensed with for certain research, including clinical trials involving a comparison of two different treatments in patients suffering from fatal diseases.[108] Instead, it is argued that investigators should "sensitively and sympathetically" explain to patients the nature of their illness, the therapeutic options available, and the objects of the research programme. If the research is not directly related to the patient's illness, its aims in helping others should be adequately outlined. Because this approach is felt to accord with good clinical practice it is suggested that there is no reason why research practices should differ.[109]

Robert Levine argues that human subject research regulation is an inevitable result of unethical research practices and the prevailing social and political conditions in the United States during the sixties and seventies. During that period, notions of individual rights and equality were coupled with anti-authoritarian sentiments which resulted in mistrust of all forms of authority. Levine suggests that this political climate fostered an "ethic of strangers" in which respect for rules which protect against arbitrary behaviour is paramount.[110] Against this background, standards requiring informed consent and review by institutional committee were promulgated to "assure a respect for rules and to guard against abuses of discretionary power".[111] However, consent regulations may in fact be a double-edged sword as the detailed documentation of consent required by the American regulations is thought to provide an effective shield against litigation.[112]

Theological perspectives

Like Robert Levine, Stanley Hauerwas regards informed consent rules as indispensable procedural safeguards which were devised in response to a lack of common values in society.[113] Hauerwas suggests that a polarization exists between those for whom the moral justification for human subject research is a matter of providing adequate information on risks and benefits, and those who argue that this approach does not satisfy the basic commitments of respect and protection for each individual.[114] Accordingly, the central issue is to determine the risks which individuals should be willing to undergo to further the well-being of the community.[115] Because the current debate fails to address this issue, he believes that a new sense of political community and resulting ethical theory must be developed which would aid the identification of the ends and values science should serve. The articulation of such ends may assist individuals in determining why they should be willing to serve as research subjects for the communal good.[116]

Hauerwas does not agree that informed consent adequately protects participants in therapeutic and non-therapeutic experimentation because of the difficulty of obtaining a genuine consent given the complexity of medical knowledge. Even if it were possible to obtain a genuine informed choice, he believes that this would not be sufficient to justify human experimentation. Because individuals can voluntarily misuse themselves, it would still be necessary to determine whether they should expose themselves to certain risks of moral and physical harm.[117] Even if informed consent could be developed into an acceptable criterion for human experimentation, problems concerning vulnerable research populations would still exist. The disadvantaged position of certain groups, such as the poor and prisoners, means that any consent they give, despite safeguards, is inherently coercive.[118]

Hauerwas disagrees with the idea that the purpose of informed consent is to create a partnership in which the subject identifies with and shares in the researcher's aims and objectives.[119] Even if one were to accept that informed consent is based on a commitment to a relationship with others, Hauerwas queries how this commitment can exist between researcher and subject in non-therapeutic research settings. Such a relationship, he contends, is not a joint venture for the good of society. Instead, it is more appropriately characterized as "a relationship of strangers" in which a significant power imbalance is justified for scientific ends.[120]

The inappropriateness of characterizing the research relationship as a joint venturer is not an exclusively theological idea. Certain medical, legal and philosophical perspectives regard the notion as detrimental to patients' interest because subjects may not understand that the element of personal care which characterizes the clinical relationship is not the sole underlying objective of research. A discussion about common aims may consequently only serve to confuse prospective subjects by obscuring conflicts of interest. Instead, decision-making may be enhanced by emphasising differences rather than "papering them over with talk of a complete commonality of concerns".[121]

Feminist perspectives

The use of women as experimental subjects and the role of informed consent has been debated in relation to reproductive technology. Some feminists seek to direct the informed consent debate away from a focus on autonomy and rights towards a consideration of how the exercise of individual rights affects the community. Robyn Rowland argues that the liberal feminist focus on autonomy and rights in the context of In Vitro Fertilization (IVF) technology is detrimental to women's interests. This is because theories concerning informed consent about a woman's right to participate in an IVF programme are based on principles of autonomy and self-determination. The individualism which these principles emphasise, overlooks the social implications of this technology on women as a group.[122] Rowland contends that feminist debate on issues such as abortion and contraception incorporates a rights rhetoric in which arguments about the right to choose are essentially concerned with the right to control one's body. It is therefore necessary to ask whether the choice to embark on an IVF programme will increase women's control over their lives or over the technology.[123] She concludes that it does neither because, in addition to any immediate physical or psychological risks to programme participants, IVF technology threatens female autonomy and control over reproduction.

Increased male control over women's reproduction is detrimental to women's social status and power which is linked to women's procreativity. For this reason, the choice of individual women to avail themselves of IVF technology places women as a group at risk of alienation from the procreative process.[124] For Rowland, the choice to embark on an IVF programme is not a voluntary action, but rather is a response to a socially constructed need. Maternal consciousness, shaped by the pro-natalist ideology of society, is conditioned to be responsive to the solutions offered by medical technology.[125] Rowland understands the appeal of autonomy for women because it has been traditionally denied them in most aspects of their lives. Claims based on individualism and free choice, she believes, must nevertheless be balanced against the interests of the community. Individual rights should not be considered in isolation from their impact on women as a social group and society in general. Whilst feminism has underscored the right of each woman to fulfil her potential, it has also stressed accountability and the need to foster women as a social group.[126] Choice should not only depend upon information concerning risks and benefits. It must be considered in terms of the political and social context in which it is made.[127] Recognizing the importance of fully informing women of the risks, outcomes and implications of reproductive technology, Rowland doubts whether an informed consent in this sense is possible to obtain. Moreover, she believes that the legal concept of informed consent is threatening to women's interests in so far as it may be used to validate experimental research which gives medical science control over women's bodies and which uses women as" living laboratories". [128]

Rowland's arguments are rejected by those for whom a right to reproductive autonomy is paramount. These individuals argue that autonomy implies a right to make one's own decisions, no matter how inappropriate or irrational they may appear to others. Moreover, a pervasive pronatalist ideology does not render women incapable of reasoned choice concerning child bearing. Rather, the social pressures and ideologies impacting upon women are factors to be considered by an individual when making a decision.[129] Legal controls are accepted as necessary both to ensure safety and to facilitate choice by requiring adequate information to be made available to women participating in IVF programmes.[130] These contrasting perspectives suggest a choice between permitting unrestricted access to reproductive technologies, thereby allowing women to be used in an experimental fashion, or depriving infertile women of a chance to bear children.[131] One suggestion for resolving this conflict includes the development of, and access to, reproductive policy that genuinely reflects women's needs, whilst respecting the interests of women and children. Pursuant to such an agenda, feminists would be encouraged to take responsibility for research into the development and regulation of reproductive technology to free it from its "patriarchal and misogynist origins".[132]

THEORIES AND VIEWS ON RESEARCH ETHICS COMMITTEES

Debate about research ethics committees largely concerns the need for a theoretical framework relating to the objectives and functions of these bodies, together with issues of interest representation. Because of the similarity of argument devised by lawyers, bioethicists, and consumerists, these viewpoints are not presented separately, although at times, reference is made to particular perspectives.

The basic task of research ethics committees is to ensure that research subjects are protected from harm during the course of research. To this end, it is the responsibility of review committees to ensure an independent determination of the rights and welfare of research subjects, the appropriateness of the methods of obtaining informed consent, and of risk-benefit evaluation. Robert Veatch argues that, although these committees are frequently referred to as "subject protection committees" they are required to balance the welfare of research participants against the anticipated benefits to society. He believes that if the sole function of these committees is the protection of subjects, a balancing of other interests seems inappropriate.[133]

A prioritizing of committee functions is contained in NHMRC guidelines. These provide that individual research subject's rights must take precedence over expected benefits to human knowledge or the community. Despite this explicit statement, IECs may not perceive their primary function as the protection of research subjects. Because the committee system was established by the NHMRC, which is the main research funding body, it has been suggested that committees may adopt a pragmatic view of the protection issue. Such pragmatism could take the form of committees keeping regulations to a minimum and promoting research to the community.[134]

The rationale for the inclusion of lay representatives on research ethics committees is that research ought no longer be subject to purely scientific evaluation, but should also be assessed according to the community's sense of proper conduct. In a pluralist society, the range of views on various issues is potentially very great. Even if particular views could be identified with specific interest groups, problems remain as to whether these views can be adequately represented. A broad spectrum of political and philosophical perspectives exist within interest groups. It will therefore be extremely difficult, if not impossible, to find a sufficiently representative person, or persons, who can, with any authenticity, claim to speak on behalf of a particular group. The impossibility of representing all views, or of identifying an individual who can provide perspectives of all the communities from which research subjects might be recruited, has led some medical commentators to advocate abandoning the idea of achieving a truly representative committee. Instead, they suggest that where community views are sought, other means of consultation should be employed.[135] From a consumer perspective, the importance of lay members is that they are in the best position to represent the interests of research participants because they will not have an interest in the research findings nor will they feel a need to "protect or promote any particular professional groups or projects".[136] In particular, they should be able to assess the adequacy of the information provided in order to determine whether the participants will be in a position to give an informed consent.[137]

The effectiveness of lay representation has been queried on the basis that the compositional requirements of ethics committees give rise to the possibility of professional dominance on these bodies. Because professionals belong to a special group which is unique in terms of its socio-economic status, ethnicity and gender, they bring a special perspective to bear on experimentation. In the case of medical researchers, this is a unique commitment to the value of research. Because of this perspective, professionals lack the competence to judge what information a reasonable lay person would require in order to give an informed consent.[138] In addition to ensuring that participants will be in a position to give an informed consent, committees must balance the welfare and rights of subjects against the benefits to the subject and society. Robert Veatch argues that risk-benefit evaluation must be judged on the basis of the reasonable person and not on the standard of the one committed to the research enterprise, unless scientists become subjects.[139]

Attention has been drawn to the practical difficulty of lay participation in medical decision-making in an Australian context. As a general rule, the only members of IECs who are independent of an institution are not medically qualified. It appears that such members seldom contribute to the analysis of medical issues involved in reviewing research proposals, thus bringing into question the independence of the review process.[140] This observation is consistent with findings of American studies on the role of lay representatives which suggest that these members may be "too easily captured" by professional members. Further, due to a lack of scientific expertise, they may be less capable of comprehending and assessing research protocols than scientific members. Consequently, it is suggested that lay members have no power to influence the outcome of decisions and no assurance that their concerns will be incorporated in the final decision.[141]

While both professional and representative skills are essential for sound decision-making, a difficulty lies in ensuring that the two are satisfactorily balanced. Robert Veatch argues that in the unlikely event that a combination of professionals who could represent the views of the reasonable person is discovered, "the egalitarianism and dignity of the layperson would be challenged by the professionalization of the reasonable person". In research ethics committees as presently composed, it is impossible to neutralize the professional bias. Alternative measures are required because the addition of community or lay representatives can only dilute but not eliminate systematic biases.[142] The notion of professional dominance has been challenged by an Australian legal commentator who argues that even where an ethics committee is composed predominantly of medical researchers, its objectivity is not automatically compromised.[143] This is because such bodies now operate in a different socio-economic climate than that which previously prevailed. The consequences for an IEC approving an unethical research project include adverse publicity, institutional liability and the jeopardising of future funding. External economic and legal forces demand that ethics committees "operate in a more impartial and balanced manner" which serves the interests of the wider community, as well as those of the research establishment.[144]

OVERVIEW

The purpose of human subject research regulation in Australia and the United States is to ensure the safety, autonomy and dignity of research subjects. International concern about harm to research participants, in the absence of adequate safeguards, was aroused by reports of Nazi atrocities during the Second World War. In the United States, the political climate of the times, together with publicity surrounding a number of unethical research practices involving vulnerable groups, prompted changes in public attitudes towards medical beneficence and paternalism. As a result, trust between subjects and investigators was no longer deemed sufficient protection for research participants. Following Congressional hearings, detailed administrative regulations governing research practices were enacted. In contrast, non-legislative guidelines were implemented in Australia. The recently-devised TGA guidelines represent the most satisfactory attempt to date to balance the needs of research subjects in terms of safety with principles of self-determination. Nevertheless, Australian standards remain deficient in a number of respects which are outlined below.

Informed consent standards

It will be recalled that in the United States, the reasonable patient standard adopted by the National Commission continues to govern disclosure in research. In Australia, it is not clear whether this standard, or the reasonable doctor standard, governs research practices. No precedents exist at common law involving disclosure practices in a research context. Guidance may be obtained from decisions concerning clinical disclosure. In this area, Australian courts have indicated that the test is not to be decided solely from a practitioner's perspective. Instead, a practitioner must provide the type of information which a reasonable doctor would give a reasonable patient, in the circumstances of the particular patient. In determining the scope of the duty, Australian courts have indicated that the amount of disclosure must be commensurate with the risk involved. According to Chief Justice King, "the more drastic the proposed intervention in the patient's physical make-up the more necessary it is to keep him fully informed as to the risks and likely consequences of the intervention".[145] Patients must be made aware of any "real risks of misfortune inherent in a particular treatment, together with any real risk that the treatment may prove ineffective".[146]

NHMRC and TGA guidelines require that research subjects are provided with information about the proposed investigation including its purpose, methods, demands, risks, inconveniences and discomforts. These guidelines fail to indicate whether the adequacy of information is to be determined from a subject or investigator perspective. The NHMRC requirement of the inclusion of lay representatives on committees, together with the directive that local, cultural and social attitudes be taken into account in decision-making, indicates an intention not to rely exclusively on professional determination of disclosure practices. There is a need to revise TGA and NHMRC guidelines taking into account common law precedents and the previously discussed draft NHMRC guidelines concerning disclosure standards in the clinical relationship.

Therapeutic privilege and waiver

It is not clear whether the so-called therapeutic privilege (the discretionary withholding of information by doctors) is permissible under the TGA and NHMRC guidelines. Nor do the guidelines indicate whether prospective subjects should be permitted to waive the opportunity to receive information. Although waiver is permitted in a clinical relationship, there are good reasons to suggest why different considerations should apply to research. The better approach would appear to be that, because of the risk factor in experimentation and because, in some circumstances, research is not intended to benefit the subject, prospective participants should always be provided with adequate information. Once advised, they will be in a position to choose to forget or ignore the information provided.[147]

Research ethics committees

Because the membership of IRBs is predominantly scientific, some feel that these bodies cannot satisfactorily determine information needs of the reasonable lay person. These concerns have been raised in the American context where the reasonable person standard of risk disclosure prevails. They are no less relevant to the Australian situation where uncertainty exists as to the nature and scope of the appropriate disclosure standard. The composition of IRBs has been criticized for failing to reflect the cultural and ethnic diversity of research populations.[148] If lay representation on IECs is to be more than mere window dressing and if requirements to take social and cultural attitudes into account in decision-making is to be given some weight, a number of issues including the selection of committee members, the range of interests they should represent, and reporting mechanisms must be addressed.

FDA advisory committee model

A suitable model is to be found in the selection of consumer representatives to FDA advisory committees. A consortium of consumer organizations with diverse representational interests is responsible for recruiting, screening, and recommending individuals to serve on advisory committees. Nominations for consumer representatives are referred to the consortium for rating in accordance with selection criteria, which include scientific knowledge, analytical and communication skills and established links with consumer and community organizations. Consortium recommendations are forwarded to the appropriate FDA staff for final selection. The consortium also plays an important role in ensuring the effectiveness of representation by establishing the accountability of representatives through performance evaluations and participation in skills training programmes.[149]

The lack of avenues for reporting unethical decision-making or an excessive stifling of research needs to be addressed. The MREC viewed IECs as autonomous bodies and did not consider it appropriate to impose reporting requirements because of the workload involved.[150] At the date of writing, it is not known whether the Health Ethics Advisory committee which succeeds the MREC will continue its policies in this regard. It is important that the work of IECs does not remain behind closed doors. Committees should therefore be required to publish their decisions which would serve as useful precedents for other IECs.

Striking a balance in regulatory policies

Human subject research regulation involves balancing a number of assumptions. The first concerns the role of rules. For some, rules protecting research subjects promote hostility between the parties. This is inimical to the development of trust and in turn threatens the "joint venture" between researchers and subjects. For others, this characterization of the research relationship is inappropriate, particularly in the case of non-therapeutic experimentation. Because parties are strangers to each other, rules are necessary to protect the interests of the weaker party. The existence of rules may mean that trust can, in part, be based on a reliance that such rules will be observed.[151] It is this consumer protection perspective which has prompted governments in both Australia and the United States to implement research controls. Ultimately, the effectiveness of the research establishment in protecting human subjects depends upon the integrity of all those involved. It is clear that even the most carefully designed regulatory system cannot provide an absolute safeguard against research abuses. Nevertheless, this knowledge should not deter governments from ensuring that regulatory controls are adequate to protect the safety, autonomy and dignity of research subjects.

Striking a balance between the protective role of government and individual self-determination is of course the tricky part. Tensions between competing assumptions of this nature are evident in the development of the concept of informed consent. Voluntary consent agreements have been criticized because they promote self-determination at the expense of values highlighting the interdependence of individuals. Certain feminist and theological perspectives focus on the vulnerability of particular research populations whose interests they regard as threatened by the notion of informed consent. Some feminists would limit an individual woman's free choice because of its effect on women as a group, and on the community. According to one theological perspective, given the vulnerability of particular groups, and because individuals can voluntarily misuse themselves, there is a need to determine what risks we should be willing to undertake to further the interests of our community.

Those who seek to limit autonomy in the interests of community, are immediately confronted by the moral, political and cultural diversity of our secular, pluralist society. Even within identifiable interest groups within the larger community there is a diversity of moral views. Consequently, attempts to argue against the exercise of choice on the basis of an appeal to community must take account of this diversity. Assuming that some degree of moral consensus is attainable, there remains a need to determine in what circumstances, if any, individual rights are entitled to prevail over those of the community. This issue has recently arisen regarding access to unapproved treatments or drugs by HIV/AIDS and cancer sufferers. The following chapter describes the way in which the demands of these groups is prompting a re-thinking of the health obligations of government and the limits of individual rights.

Notes

1. Declaration of Helsinki - Recommendations Guiding Medical Doctors in Biomedical Research involving Human Subjects as revised by the 29th World Medical Assembly, Tokyo, Japan, 1975.
2. Levine R., Ethics and Regulation of Clinical Research. Urban and Schwarzenberg 1986,129.
3. Medical Research Council (Canada) Ethical Considerations in research involving human subjects. MRC Ottawa 1978.
4. 45 CFR 46.405. Levine, Ethics and Regulation of Clinical Research, op.cit. 8-10.
5. Fried C., Medical Experimentation: Personal Integrity and Social Policy. North Holland Publishing Company 1974, 30-1.
6. Annas G., Faith (Healing), Hope and Charity at the FDA: The Politics of AIDS Drug Trials. 34 Villanova Law Review 1989, 771, 789.
7. Id.791, n.63.
8. In a clinical trial based on historical controls, control data are obtained from the experience in treating the disease in question accumulated up to the introduction of the new drug. Annas, op.cit. 791, n.64. For a discussion of the circumstances in which placebo-controlled RTC's may be justified see Levine C. Neveloff Dubler N. and Levine R., Building a New Consensus: Ethical Principles and Policies for Clinical Research on HIV/AIDS. 13 IRB: A Review of Human Subjects Research 1991, 1, 8.
9. Faden R. and Beauchamp T., A History and Theory of Informed Consent. Oxford University Press 1986, 205.
10. Greenwald R. Ryan M. and Mulvihill J., Human Subjects Research - A Handbook for Institutional Review Boards. Plenum Press 1982, 5.
11. Faden and Beauchamp, op.cit. 205.
12. Beecher H.K., Ethics and Clinical Research. 274 New England Journal of Medicine 1966, 1354.
13. Faden and Beauchamp, op.cit. 159, 163.
14. Beecher, op.cit.; Faden and Beauchamp, op.cit. 159.
15. Faden and Beauchamp, op.cit. 162.
16. Id.164.
17. For a more detailed discussion of these research abuses see Faden and

Beauchamp, op.cit. 161-7. See in particular Jones J.H., Bad Blood - The Tuskegee Syphilis Experiment. The Free Press 1981.

18. Greenwald et al., op. cit. 5-6, 13-7.
19. Id.5-6. Faden and Beauchamp, op. cit. 214.
20. For a discussion of the role of these agencies see Curran W., Governmental Regulation of the Use of Human Subjects in Medical Research: The Approach of Two Federal Agencies. 98 Daedalus 1969, 542.
21. 21 U.S.C.s321(g)(1). The FDA is empowered to regulate the marketing and promotion of prescription drugs pursuant to the provisions of the Food Drug and Cosmetic Act 1938 (as amended).
22. 21 U.S.C. s.355 (a)(b)and (d).
23. 21 U.S.C.s.355(1) 1982.
24. Kessler D., The Regulation of Investigational Drugs. 320 New England Journal of Medicine 1989, 282.
25. Id.281-2.
26. Id.281.
27. 21 CFR s.312.21.
28. Levine, Neveloff Dubler and Levine, op.cit. 4.
29. Kessler, op.cit. 282.
30. In 1967, more stringent consent regulations were enacted. These regulations distinguish between therapeutic and non-therapeutic research. In the former case, consent is required in all but exceptional cases. It is always required in relation to non-therapeutic research. 32 F.R.8753, June 20 1967; 21 CFR 130.37.
31. Kessler, op.cit. 283.
32. Darvall L., Consumer Participation in Government Decisionmaking: New Drug Evaluation in Australia and the United States. 6 Journal of Consumer Policy 1986, 41,43.
33. Ibid. See also text at n.28 above.
34. Kessler, op.cit. 283.
35. Areen J. King P. Goldberg S. and Capron A., Law, Science and Medicine. University Casebook Series, Foundation Press 1984, 960.
36. Starr P., The Social Transformation of American Medicine. Basic Books Inc. 1982, 340-2.
37. Levine, Ethics and Regulation of Clinical Research, op.cit. 322.
38. Faden and Beauchamp, op.cit. 202.
39. Veatch R., Human experimentation committees : professional or representative. 5 Hastings Center Report 1975, 31, 32.
40. Gillespie R., Research on Human Subjects: An Historical Overview. 8 Bioethics News 1989, 4,11.
41. Levine, Ethics and Regulation of Clinical Research, op.cit. 323.
42. Rothman D. Strangers at the Bedside - A History of How Law and Bioethics Transformed Medical Decision Making. Basic Books 1991, 90-1.
43. Id.91.
44. Id.92.
45. Veatch, op.cit. 33.
46. Ibid.

47. Faden and Beauchamp, op.cit. 212 n. 45.
48. Id.212.
49. Id.213.
50. Veatch, op.cit. 34.
51. Faden and Beauchamp, op.cit. 214.
52. Id.214-5.
53. Id.215 - 6.
54. Veatch, op.cit. 34.
55. Levine, Ethics and the Regulation of Clinical Research, op.cit. 15.
56. Faden and Beauchamp, op.cit. 216.
57. Levine, Ethics and Regulation of Clinical Research, op.cit. 16.
58. The National Commission for the Protection of Human Subjects of Biomedical and Behavioral Research.1978. Institutional Review Boards: Report and Recommendations. DHEW Publications No.(OS)78-0008. Washington D.C.
59. Faden and Beauchamp, op.cit. 216.
60. Levine R., Protection of Human Subjects of Biomedical Research in the United States, in Biomedical Ethics: An Anglo-American Dialogue 530 Annals of the New York Academy of Sciences 1985, 135-6.
61. Levine, The Ethics and Regulation of Clinical Research, op.cit. 17.
62. Id.17-18.
63. Greenwald, op.cit. 14.
64. Levine, Ethics and Regulation of Clinical Research op.cit. 15.
65. Capron A.M., Human Experimentation in Medical Ethics, in Veatch R.(ed.), Medical Ethics. Jones and Bartlett 1989, 127, 141-2.
66. Department of Health and Human Services Rules and Regulations, 45 CFR s.46.111a.1983.
67. Levine R., Institutional Review Boards 298 British Medical Journal 1989, 1268-9.
68. 45 CFR Part 46, s.46.116 Federal Register January 26,1981.
69. 45 CFR s.46.116 1983.
70. Greenwald, op.cit. 159.
71. 45 CFR s.46.107 1983.
72. Levine, Neveloff Dubler and Levine, op.cit. 3.
73. Levine, Institutional Review Boards, op.cit. 1268-9.
74. Levine, Neveloff Dubler and Levine, op.cit. 3.
75. Faden and Beauchamp, op. cit. 223.
76. Veatch R., Two Views of the New Research Regulations. 1 Hastings Center Report 1981, 9, 12.
77. NHMRC 1976, Supplementary Note 1.
78. Medical Research Ethics Committee Report on Workshops on the Constitution and Functions of Institutional Ethics Committees in Australia, 1984-5. 1985, 2. (Hereinafter referred to as Medical Research Ethics Committee Report).
79. Laufer S., The Regulation of Medical/Scientific Research Practices Involving Experimentation on Human Beings. 8 Law in Context 1990,78, 80.
80. Medical Research Ethics Committee Report, op.cit. 3.
81. The NHMRC adopted these revised guidelines in 1985 and recommended to the Minister of Health that it should be a condition of an award of research funds

that all applications after January 1, 1986 should be approved by an IEC constituted and functioning in accordance with the guidelines.

82. Australian Bureau of Statistics. 1986-7. Research and experimental development, all sector summary, Australia, Canberra ABS, 1989.
83. NHMRC Statement on Human Experimentation and Supplementary Notes 1985, 1.
84. Ibid.
85. Ibid.
86. McNeill P. Berglund C. and Webster W., Reviewing the reviewers: a survey of institutional ethics committees in Australia. 152 Medical Journal of Australia 1990, 289.
87. Id.290.
88. Id.292.
89. Id.294.
90. Recent TGA guidelines require that committee members who have an interest in the outcome of a study not vote on any proposal in which they are personally interested. Guidelines for Good Clinical Research Practice (GCRP) in Australia 1991 2.1.9, 5.1.(Hereinafter referred to as TGA Guidelines for Good Clinical Research Practice).
91. McNeill, Berglund and Webster, op.cit. 294. Recent TGA guidelines state that monitoring of trials by the IEC which granted approval or an individual monitor is expected. TGA Guidelines for Good Clinical Research Practice, op.cit. 5.2, 5.3, 10.
92. Mc Neill, Berglund and Webster, op.cit. 296.
93. TGA Guidelines for Good Clinical Research Practice, op.cit. The Therapeutic Goods Administration of the Commonwealth Department of Health, Housing and Community Services is the regulatory agency responsible for reviewing clinical studies. The TGA guidelines are based upon the Declaration of Helsinki and the NHMRC Statement on Human Experimentation and Supplementary notes and should be read in conjunction with these documents.
94. This accords with a recommendation of the AIDS Council of New South Wales (ACON). The Trailing, Approval and Marketing of Treatment and Therapies for HIV /AIDS and Related Illness in Australia - A Policy Document 1990 rec.2.10.
95. TGA Guidelines for Good Clinical Research Practice, op.cit.
96. Canterbury v Spence, 464 F 2d 72, CA DC 1972.
97. Halushka v University of Saskatchewan CA (1965) 53 DLR (2d) 436.
98. Cartwright S.R., The committee of enquiry into allegations concerning the of cervical cancer at National Women's Hospital and into other related matters. The report of the cervical cancer inquiry. Auckland: Government Printing Office 1988, as cited in McNeill P., The Implications for Australia of the New Zealand Report of The Cervical Cancer Inquiry: No Cause For Complacency. 150 Medical Journal of Australia 1989, 264, 267; Coney S., The Unfortunate Experiment. Penguin 1988.
99. Greenwald, op.cit. 159.
100. Fried C., Medical Experimentation: Personal Integrity and Social Policy. North Holland Publishing Company 1974, 53.
101. Id.54.

102. Id.56.
103. Beecher H.K., Consent in Clinical Experimentation: Myth and Reality. 195 Journal of the American Medical Association 124-5, 1966 as cited in Appelbaum P.S. Lidz C.W. and Meisel J.D., Informed Consent - Legal Theory and Clinical Practice. Oxford University Press 1987, 242.
104. Ingelfinger F. Informed (but uneducated) Consent. 1972 287 New England Journal of Medicine 465 - 6.
105. Ibid.
106. Ibid.
107. Weatherall D.J., Commentary. 8 Journal of Medical Ethics 1982, 63..
108. Lewis P.J., The Drawback of Research Ethics Committees. 8 Journal of Medical Ethics 1982, 61,62. Weatherall, op.cit. 63, 64.
109. Weatherall, op.cit. 64.
110. Levine, Protection of Human Subjects of Biomedical Research in the United States, op.cit. 134.
111. Id.135.
112. Levine, Ethics and Regulation of Clinical Research, op.cit. 134.
113. Hauerwas S., Suffering Presence - Theological Reflections on Medicine, the Mentally Handicapped, and the Church. University of Notre Dame Press 1986, 117.
114. Id.114-5.
115. Ibid.
116. Ibid.
117. Id.119-20.
118. Id.120.
119. Such an interpretation of the researcher-subject relationship has been developed by Paul Ramsey, amongst others. Ramsey P., The Patient as Person. Yale University Press 1977, 5-6, as cited in Appelbaum, Lidz and Meisel, op.cit. 241.
120. Hauerwas, op.cit. 122-3.
121. Appelbaum, Lidz and Meisel, op.cit. 242.
122. Rowland R., Choice, Control and Issues of Informed Consent: The New Reproductive and Pre-Birth Technologies. Informed Consent Symposia, Law Reform Commission of Victoria 1988, 102.
123. Id.103.
124. Ibid.
125. Id.106-8.
126. Id.104.
127. For a similar analysis see Sherwin S., Feminist and Medical Ethics: Two Different Approaches to Contextual Ethics in Feminist Perspectives in Medical Ethics. Holmes H.B. and Purdy L. (eds). Indiana University Press 1992,17.
128. Rowland, op.cit. 102.
129. Warren M., IVF and Women's Interests: An Analysis of Feminists Concerns. 2 Bioethics 1988, 37, 41.
130. Id.40.
131. Overall C., Ethics and Human Reproduction - A Feminist Analysis. Allen and Unwin 1987, 203.

132. Id.205.
133. Veatch R., Human experimentation committees: professional or representative? 5 Hastings Center Report 1975, 31,35.
134. Osborne L. W., Research on human subjects: Australian ethics committees take tentative steps. 9 Journal of Medical Ethics 1983, 66,68.
135. Levine, Ethics and Regulation of Clinical Research, op.cit. 355-6; Nolan K.A., Student Members "Informed Outsiders" on IRBs. 2 IRB: Review of Human Subjects Research 1980, 1,2.
136. Krestensen C., Clinical Trials in Australia - The Role of Institutional Ethics Committees 11 Health Forum 1989, 11.
137. Herxheimer A., The Rights of the Patient in Clinical Research. The Lancet, 1988 1128 as cited in Krestensen, op.cit. 11.
138. Veatch, op.cit. 36-7.
139. Id.38.
140. McNeill, Berglund and Webster op.cit. 264, 271.
141. Laufer, op.cit. 87.
142. Veatch, op.cit. 37.
143. Drahos P., Regulating Reproductive Technology: The Role of Ethics Committees. 11 Australian Health Review 1988, 88.
144. Id.88-9.
145. F v R (1983) 33 S.A.S.R. 189 at 192.
146. Id.191.
147. Levine, Ethics and Regulation of Clinical Research, op.cit. 105.
148. Levine, Neveloff Dubler and Levine, op.cit. 3, 11.; Spiers H., Community Consultation and AIDS Clinical Trials: 13 IRB - A Review of Human Subjects Research 1991, Part 3, 5.
149. Darvall L.W., Consumer Participation in Government Decisionmaking: New Drug Evaluation in Australia and the United States. 6 Journal of Consumer Policy 1986, 41,46.
150. Krestensen, op.cit. 11.
151. Childress J., Who Should Decide? Paternalism in Health Care. Oxford University Press, 48.

5 Recent Developments in Human Subject Research Regulation in Australia and The United States

INTRODUCTION

Securing legislative rights of safety and information and establishing a system of participatory decision-making were early concerns of the consumer movement. Governments in Australia and America responded to these demands. Following the thalidomide tragedy, amendments to the U.S. Federal Food Drug and Cosmetic Act required, amongst other things, proof of a drug's efficacy in addition to its safety. Throughout the following decades, FDA regulations and evaluation procedures were criticized by industry, as well as by members of the scientific establishment. Criticism largely concerned the amount of documentation necessary to meet FDA statutory requirements. In particular, the volume of material required to support a new drug application was identified as a factor which contributed to delays in granting marketing approval. Because of lengthy FDA evaluation procedures, it was suggested that American consumers were denied the benefits of certain drugs available for use in other countries, with less stringent regulations. Despite these criticisms, the notion prevailed in Congress and elsewhere, that the FDA is responsible for protecting the public from untoward effects of drug products. This mandate was interpreted by legislators and administrators alike as justifying a cautious regulatory approach. Consumer groups endorsed the protectionist stance of the FDA because of the possibility of serious injury which may result from the use of drug products. An additional reason for their support was that some drugs which had not been approved in the United States, but which had been approved elsewhere, were subsequently banned following discovery of serious side-effects undetected during pre-approval clinical studies.[1]

From 1962, until the beginning of the eighties, there were no formal procedures governing access to investigational drugs. During the sixties, the FDA developed an informal policy of compassionate use which permitted individual doctors access to experimental drugs for seriously ill patients. Physicians who obtained drugs on this basis were not treated as investigators, nor were they subject to stringent monitoring requirements. Additional expanded access policies were developed during the seventies. Sponsors of controlled trials were permitted to develop concurrent open label safety studies. Thousand of patients received, and are continuing to receive, access to experimental drugs at various stages of investigation as a result of these studies. Despite sponsors being required by the FDA to collect safety data, it is widely believed that the primary purpose of these studies is to provide therapy to patients. Increased access to certain investigational cancer drugs distributed by the National Cancer Institute has been made possible by virtue of a Group C cancer drug IND.[2] In 1983, FDA procedures were revised in order to reduce the time taken for approving new drugs. By this time, public perception of the research enterprise as one of high risk was changing as a result of the small number of subjects actually injured in the course of experimentation.[3]

Until the early eighties, key participants in the debate over FDA regulatory policy included members of the scientific community, industry representatives and consumer groups. Individuals denied early access to drugs because of FDA regulatory delays do not appear to have been part of this debate. A possible explanation is that these individuals were not organized politically, and with few exceptions, were unaware of their plight.[4] Some however, were sufficiently motivated to turn to the courts in order to gain access to unapproved drugs and treatments. During the eighties, there were increasing demands on American and Australian health authorities for greater access to unapproved drugs and therapies. In particular, pressure has come from cancer patients, and since the mid-eighties, from people with AIDS (PWAs). Largely in response to the AIDS crisis, governments both in the United States and Australia developed policies on a variety of issues, including access to unapproved drugs. In this chapter, unconventional cancer treatments are discussed together with three American cases concerning access to and the use of unapproved cancer treatments. The demands of gay rights and AIDS activists together with recent modifications in American and Australian human subject research regulatory policy are subsequently discussed.

ACCESS TO UNAPPROVED CANCER TREATMENTS

Types of unconventional cancer treatments

The majority of American cancer sufferers do not use unconventional treatments.[5] Nevertheless, a recent report by the U.S. Office of Technology Assessment estimates that each year thousands of cancer patients use treatments not accepted by mainstream medicine.[6] Unconventional cancer treatments are generally undertaken by scientists and physicians in private clinics with the aim of patient care rather than experimental research. As such they are not subject to institutional constraints, including IRB review.[7] There is a wide range of these treatments, some of which can be used in conjunction with conventional treatments. Others, either because of their nature, or because of the individuals who dispense them, are used exclusive of orthodox medicine. Unconventional treatments classified as drugs must conform with FDA safety and efficacy standards. Attempts to evade these standards, or failure to conform can lead to the imposition of a wide range of civil and criminal sanctions. FDA regulation extends to pharmacologic agents such as laetrile, biologic products, herbal and homeopathic preparations. Other types of unconventional treatments, such as nutritional regimens and psychological or life style approaches, are not within FDA control.[8] FDA regulations governing drug evaluation, approval and promotion, do not extend to medical practice. Once a drug is approved, the FDA has no control over whether practitioners prescribe it for approved or unapproved uses. Despite jurisdictional limits, it is claimed that the FDA has attempted to prevent doctors from using unconventional treatments, especially those offering alternative approaches to cancer.[9]

Reasons for the use of unconventional cancer treatments

Interest in unapproved treatments appears to stem largely from a dissatisfaction with orthodox medical procedures. Among cancer patients, a strong correlation is reported between experienced toxicity from standard treatments and subsequent use of unapproved treatments.[10] In addition to a hopeful prognosis, some cancer patients seek supportive and caring attention, which they believe is absent from orthodox medical practice.[11] Others are concerned that orthodox treatment, even if successful, may result in an impaired quality of life. In contrast to mainstream research, quality of life features prominently as an objective in unorthodox treatments. While mainstream researchers have begun including quality of life assessments in clinical trials, the emphasis is on anti-tumour effects rather than on improved quality of life for cancer patients.[12] Resort to unconventional cancer treatment may also be due to scientific as well as lay criticism of the success rate of conventional cancer treatments. The U.S.National Cancer Institute's (NCI) cancer survival statistics has been disputed in a recent report by a Congressional agency. In each case, the agency found a more modest improvement than NCI, or none at all. The publication of these results initiated public debate about cancer treatment. It also prompted NCI to establish a panel of technical experts and lay representatives to make recommendations on appropriate measures for assessing progress in cancer treatment.[13]

Medical and government attitudes towards unapproved treatments

Research involving unconventional treatments is generally not well designed according to orthodox medical standards. A major difference between supporters of unconventional treatments and orthodox medicine concerns what constitutes acceptable evidence of benefit.[14] The development of new forms of cancer diagnosis and treatment is primarily undertaken by the PHS within the Department of Health and Human Services. The NIH, mainly through the National Cancer Institute (NCI), tests and awards grants for cancer research. The NCI conducts clinical trials involving potential new agents for the treatment of cancer. The Institute has stated its willingness to evaluate any new proposals, including those which are not supported by traditional scientific evidence.[15]

Allegations of bias have been made against public and private regulatory agencies.[16] A number of organizations, including the American Cancer Society have established committees which determine what treatments should be listed as unproven therapies. Listing in this manner can give rise to serious consequences for researchers, including denial of research funds, difficulty in publishing results, loss of peer acceptance and refusal of government co-operation.[17] Critics argue that this system is inherently biased because committees are composed of mainstream practitioners who have negative attitudes towards non-conventional therapies.[18] FDA reluctance to approve clinical testing of unorthodox cancer therapies has also been criticized. The discretion afforded to the agency under the regulations governing INDs, has allegedly permitted endless delaying tactics, amounting to a ban. From an agency perspective this stance is justified to protect the public from what, in some instances, are regarded as hoax remedies.[19]

Widespread patient demand for access to unapproved drugs prompted government evaluation of vitamin C and laetrile. By 1982, use of laetrile had been legalized in a large number of States despite the fact that it had not received FDA approval. In response to public pressure, the National Cancer Institute (NCI) undertook a multi-institutional trial to determine whether there was any evidence that it caused tumour regression. Results indicated that the drug provided no substantive benefits in terms of cure, improvement or stabilization of cancer, or extension of life span. It was also found that it produced dangerous blood levels of cyanide. On this basis it was concluded that laetrile is a toxic drug which is not effective as a cancer treatment.[20] Although laetrile proponents were critical of these tests, a 1990 report of the U.S. Office of Technology Assessment (OTA) on unorthodox cancer treatments, suggests that the study appears to have been a fair test as to whether the drug was an anti-tumour agent.[21] A willingness to encourage and facilitate evaluation of unconventional treatments is evident in the OTA report. In its list of options, the report recommended that the NCI should gather information on the range of available unconventional cancer treatments, develop guidelines to assist unconventional treatment investigators in presenting data suitable for publication in peer reviewed literature, and provide advice to unconventional practitioners on drug evaluation methodology. It also recommended Federal funding for unconventional treatment evaluation, and the establishment of a review committee comprising unconventional treatment practitioners as well as mainstream scientists.[22]

Judicial decisions concerning access to unapproved drugs for cancer treatment

A right of unrestricted access to unapproved drugs has been pursued through the American courts. To date, the decided cases endorse a policy of consumer protection, rather than a free choice approach. A recent case, Schneider v Revici, which is still pending final outcome, indicates a greater willingness on the part of courts to allow patients to assume responsibility for choosing their own treatment.

People v Privitera

In this case, Dr Privitera was charged with violating the Californian Health and Safety Code by conspiring to sell, or prescribe, the unapproved drug laetrile to cancer patients. The decision was appealed on the grounds that the legislation was unconstitutional. It was also contended that the right of privacy, protected by Federal and State Constitutions, includes a right of access to drugs which have not been approved as effective by the FDA.[23] The conviction was overturned by the California Court of Appeals on the grounds that the Californian health and safety code violates the constitutional right to privacy. On appeal to the California Supreme Court, it was held that the right to obtain drugs of unproven efficacy is not encompassed by either a Federal or State constitutional right of privacy.[24] The court distinguished the decision of the Court of Appeals in the Rutherford case (discussed below) on the grounds that the present case did not involve terminally ill patients. The court specifically indicated that its judgement should not be interpreted as a safety or efficacy assessment of the drug, observing that contemporaneous tests were being undertaken by NCI for this purpose.

In a dissenting judgement, Chief Justice Bird endorsed a patient's right of choice as follows:

> So long as there is no clear evidence that laetrile is unsafe to the user, I believe each individual patient has a right to obtain the substance from a licensed physician who feels it appropriate to prescribe it to him. Cancer is a disease with potentially fatal consequences; this makes the choice of treatment one of the more important decisions a person may ever make, touching intimately on his or her being. For this reason, I believe the right to privacy, recognized under both the state and federal Constitutions, prevents the state from interfering with a person's choice of treatment on the sole grounds that the person has chosen a treatment which the state considers "ineffective".[25]

U.S. v Rutherford

In this case, the plaintiff Glen Rutherford initially brought suit in a Federal district court, on behalf of a class of cancer patients, to stop the FDA from prohibiting interstate shipment of laetrile.[26] The court gave judgement for the plaintiffs, limiting purchase of the drug to terminally ill patients. The decision was upheld by the U.S. Court of Appeals. It was subsequently appealed and ultimately reached the U.S. Supreme Court where the issue before the court was whether the FDA safety and efficacy requirements apply to drugs for terminally ill patients. In a unanimous decision, the Supreme Court held that drugs used to treat terminally ill patients are not exempt from the marketing approval provisions of the Federal Food Drug and

Cosmetic Act. The Supreme Court stated that determining exemptions of this nature is a matter more appropriately dealt with by the legislature rather than the courts. In reaching its decision the court commented as follows:

> Only when a literal construction of a statute yields results so manifestly unreasonable that they could not fairly be attributed to Congressional design will an exception to statutory language be judicially implied. Here, however, we have no license to depart from the plain language of the Act, for Congress could reasonably have intended to shield terminal patients from ineffectual or unsafe drugs.[27]

The Supreme Court further commented:

> For the terminally ill, as for anyone else, a drug is unsafe if its potential for inflicting death or physical injury is not offset by the possibility of therapeutic benefit. .. Moreover, there is a special sense in which the relationship between drug effectiveness and safety has meaning in the context of incurable illness. An otherwise harmless drug can be dangerous to any patient if it does not produce its purported therapeutic effect. But if an individual suffering from a potentially fatal disease rejects conventional therapy in favour of a drug with no demonstrable curative properties, the consequences can be irreversible.[28]

The Supreme Court did not determine whether there was a constitutional right of privacy which rendered attempts to stop the use of laetrile unconstitutional. The case was remanded to a lower court where the argument that the right of privacy extends to the use of unapproved drugs was dismissed on the grounds that it is acceptable for a state to limit patient access to drugs. The effectiveness provision of the Federal Food Drug and Cosmetic Act was held to be a rational way to achieve this end. In reaching its decision, the court commented as follows:

> ...the decision by the patient whether to have a treatment or not is a protected right, but his selection of a particular treatment, or at least a medication, is within the area of governmental interest in protecting health.[29]

American case law establishes that unless a fundamental right is involved, a law will not be held to be unconstitutional, provided it bears a rational relationship to a legitimate government purpose.[30] Protection of public health and safety is recognized as such an end, so that unless a health law is clearly unreasonable, it will not be deemed unconstitutional. It is unlikely that patients have a constitutional right to obtain unapproved drugs on the basis of established precedent.[31] In order to succeed on this ground, it would be necessary to establish that legislative provisions denying or limiting access are irrational and bear no relationship to the legitimate purpose of promoting public health and safety. Consequently, a challenge of this nature would be unlikely to succeed where efficacy of a particular drug had not been established, and even less likely in the absence of evidence of safety.[32]

Schneider v Revici

In this case, the plaintiff sued Dr Revici for fraud and medical malpractice in treating her breast cancer with unorthodox treatments of no proven value.[33] The jury awarded Mrs Schneider one million dollars in damages in relation to her malpractice claim. This amount was subsequently reduced by fifty per cent, on the grounds that Mrs Schneider had been negligent in subjecting herself to Dr Revici's care. The defendant appealed, arguing that the trial court had erred in not permitting the defence of assumption of risk to be submitted for jury consideration. This defence, if successfully pleaded, relieves a defendant from all liability. The appeals court found for Dr Revici on this point, and remanded the case to a lower court for consideration of this issue. In reaching its decision, the appeals court observed as follows:

> [W]e see no reason why a patient should not be allowed to make an informed decision to go outside currently approved medical methods in search of an unconventional treatment. While a patient should be encouraged to exercise care for his own safety, we believe that an informed decision to avoid surgery and conventional therapy is within the patient's right "to determine what shall be done with his own body".[34]

ACCESS TO UNAPPROVED DRUGS FOR HIV/ AIDS TREATMENT

During the eighties, the HIV/AIDS crisis emerged prompting gay activists and HIV/AIDS-infected gay men to establish networks for acquiring and disseminating information about potential treatments. Established gay rights organizations joined newly-formed high-profile lobby groups in order to influence Government policies in Australia and the United States. An urgent issue for AIDS advocates and PWAs was to secure rights of unrestricted access to experimental therapies. Their demands challenged the role of drug regulatory authorities which, post-thalidomide, was interpreted by government officials as including an obligation to protect vulnerable individuals from the risks of experimentation. The desperate situation of PWAs caused AIDS groups to reject regulatory paternalism. Instead, they argued that government should not usurp their right to make decisions but should facilitate choice by providing patients with adequate information. In addition, government regulations should not require people to participate in placebo-controlled studies, or limit their ability to mix therapies. The essence of these arguments is that the interests of those currently infected with HIV/AIDS are paramount and should take precedence over the long-term interests of research and future patients.[35] In response to these demands, the FDA devised a number of procedures which are discussed below.

Recent FDA initiatives in widening access to unapproved drugs

Treatment INDs

Until 1987, access to investigational drugs, with some exceptions, was limited to subjects enrolled in a clinical trial specified in an IND.[36] Following extensive discussions between AIDS activists and FDA officials, regulations were enacted which increase the availability of promising new drugs still in the clinical pre-marketing phase. Pursuant to a treatment IND, investigational drugs that are in phase 3 trials, or in some circumstances phase 2 trials, or which are awaiting evaluation following clinical testing, are available to patients who do not have access to treatment and who are not enrolled in a clinical trial.[37] In order for a drug to be assigned treatment IND status, a number of additional criteria must be satisfied. First, it must be intended for treatment of a life threatening or serious disease. Second, there must be no comparable or satisfactory alternative drug or treatment available. Once an alternative treatment becomes available, treatment IND status is no longer available as an option.[38] Third, there must be a proper treatment protocol in place requiring the collection of certain experimental data and the drug's sponsor must be actively pursuing its marketing approval.

Treatment IND status may be denied if clinical tests have not provided promising results. In the case of a drug for the treatment of a serious illness, status may be denied if there is insufficient evidence of safety and effectiveness. For a drug for an immediately life threatening disease, a request may be denied only if there is no evidence of its efficacy, or if the FDA considers that it would expose patients to an unreasonable risk.[39] Adequate enrollment in clinical trials must also be assured before the FDA approves a treatment IND.[40] The decision to grant IND status is conditional upon compliance with certain procedural safeguards. These include obtaining the informed consent of participants, the establishment of institutional review boards, distribution of the drug by qualified experts and the submission of IND safety reports to the FDA.[41] Manufacturers of drugs with treatment IND status are entitled to charge for their use to recover research, development and handling costs. Prior to the implementation of these regulations, drug companies were not permitted to charge for drugs in clinical trials, unless special approval had been obtained.

The FDA has stated that it does not consider that the treatment IND regulations are inconsistent with the decision in the Rutherford case for the following reasons:

> The Court in Rutherford noted that application of the new drug approval provisions to therapies for terminal diseases did not foreclose resort to experimental drugs by patients for whom conventional therapy was unavailable. The Court noted that the act makes explicit provision for carefully regulated use of certain drugs not yet demonstrated safe and effective. The final rule, while permitting cost recovery for certain investigational drugs, maintains the prohibition against commercialization: distribution of a drug under an approved treatment IND/protocol, therefore, continues to be a carefully regulated distribution. Treatment use of an investigational drug is conditioned on the sponsor complying with all

the safeguards inherent in the IND process including informed consent, IRB review and the applicable provisions of Part 312, such as distribution of the drug through qualified experts, maintenance of adequate manufacturing facilities, and submission of IND safety reports.[42]

AIDS groups claim that this method of access is not satisfactory. In particular, they argue that the FDA's interpretation of the efficacy standard has been too rigorous and too similar to that applied for final approval of a drug. As a result, treatment INDs have not increased access to drugs at earlier stages of development or assisted patients ineligible for conventional clinical trials.[43] Treatment IND regulations have also been criticized by a Presidential Commission on AIDS which noted the absence of a system for informing patients and their doctors which drugs are available on a treatment IND basis. The Commission considered the methods for obtaining available drugs to be both complicated and poorly understood and observed that some doctors are reluctant to prescribe treatment IND drugs because of fear of legal liability. It also noted the unwillingness of some companies to make their drugs available on this basis.[44]

Individual import of unapproved drugs

In response to requests from HIV/AIDS patients wishing to import an unapproved drug, dextran sulfate, the FDA indicated that, for compassionate reasons, it will permit the importation of small quantities of the drug for personal use. Pursuant to this policy, evidence of safety and effectiveness is not required, provided the agency is satisfied that there is no evidence of unreasonable risk or fraud.[45] This policy has been criticized because it departs from the consumer protection perspective of the Rutherford decision.[46]

Expedited development

In 1988, the FDA implemented an expedited development process to reduce the testing time for drugs designed for the treatment of life-threatening and severely debilitating diseases. This process, which follows a pattern established by the development of the drug zidovudine, is designed to eliminate phase 3 clinical trials for drugs shown to improve survival or prevent irreversible morbidity. Procedural guidelines specify that the FDA will assist drug sponsors in devising animal and human studies which will yield safety and efficacy data in the least amount of time possible. In addition, the FDA monitors clinical trials and may also provide assistance in the development of post-marketing surveillance studies.[47]

Parallel track

This concept was first proposed by HIV/AIDS activists and was subsequently brought to public attention in 1989 by Dr Anthony Fauci, director of the National Institutes of Allergy and Infectious Diseases (NIAID). Its purpose is to expand the availability of investigational drugs at a very early stage of clinical testing. Under this system new drugs with proven safety are simultaneously available through clinical trials, and by means of expanded access to individuals ineligible for clinical trials through their physicians.[48] A parallel track protocol can be approved for a promising investigational drug when evidence of its effectiveness is less than that required for a treatment IND.[49] Guidelines for parallel track were developed by an HIV/AIDS advocacy group, AIDS Coalition To Unleash Power (ACT UP). They were subsequently endorsed by twenty AIDS groups and the FDA Anti-Viral Drugs Advisory Committee. A task force to draw up detailed recommendations was established by the National AIDS Programme Office (NAPO) which included AIDS advocacy groups, industry representatives and researchers.

A proposed policy statement on parallel track was published in May 1990, which requires promising evidence of efficacy, and evidence of reasonable safety. Additional information would be required regarding lack of satisfactory alternatives, the type of patient population and an assessment of the impact of parallel track on recruitment for clinical trials. Details would also be required of the information to be provided by a manufacturer to participating physicians and participants to ensure that they receive adequate information of potential risks and benefits.[50] Sponsors will be required to establish a data and safety monitoring board responsible for overseeing the parallel track protocol and comparing findings from parallel track with information gathered from related clinical trials.[51] Eligibility criteria outlined in the proposed policy statement include the following requirements. First, patients must have clinically significant HIV-related illness or be at imminent health risk because of HIV-related immunodeficiency. Second, patients must be ineligible to participate in controlled clinical trials due to failure to meet entry criteria, or because they are too ill, or because participation would cause undue hardship. Physicians wishing to enrol a patient in the parallel track must provide evidence that existing approved therapies are contra-indicated or ineffective or that the patient is unable to tolerate them.[52]

Whilst government initiatives described above are generally welcomed by PWAs and AIDS activists, others, including members of the medical profession and scientific establishment, have expressed some reservations concerning the overall efficacy of expanded access mechanisms. Some of these contrasting views will be outlined in a subsequent section.

Community-based clinical trials programmes

The AIDS agenda is not limited to issues of access. Compassionate treatment and care for PWAs is also an urgent need. This has prompted demands for research to be conducted outside formal research settings and involving patients' own physicians. Participatory decision-making has also assumed a prominent role in an overall strategy concerned with patient empowerment. In 1986, the AIDS clinical trials group (ACTG) was established by the National Institutes of Allergy and Infectious Diseases (NIAID) to undertake clinical and laboratory studies for the development of antiviral drugs. Clinical trials are conducted according to traditional research designs and procedures at forty-seven University-based research hospitals. AIDS groups criticized these trials on the basis that they do not include certain patient groups. An additional criticism is that many important aspects of research could be undertaken in settings lacking the technology of the ACTG institutions.[53] Community Programmes for Clinical Research on AIDS (CPCRA) was established in 1989 to redress some of the shortcomings in the ACTG system. Community care providers and their patients can participate in clinical trials at eighteen diverse centres. In particular, NIAID seeks through these centres to increase the access of hitherto underserved groups to experimental therapies.[54]

Despite government programmes, dissatisfaction with government-controlled clinical trials led to the establishment of a network of community-based clinical trial centres. These groups are more receptive to the testing of novel therapeutic approaches than the ACTG system. One such centre, the Community Research Initiative (CRI) was established in New York City in 1986 by the research arm of the People with AIDS Coalition.[55] CRI is committed to ensuring responsible scientific research and does not endorse distribution of substances of unknown safety and efficacy. To this end, it has established a scientific advisory committee composed of outstanding AIDS clinicians and scientists. This committee, together with an Advisory Committee of community-based physicians, develops protocols for HIV-related primary care. In addition, it identifies research priorities and makes recommendations on protocols to the CRI Board of Directors and IRB.[56]

As a means of fostering representative decision-making, membership of the CRI IRB includes individuals with diverse expertise in bioethics and the biosciences as well as representatives of the HIV/AIDS-affected community. To encourage each of the twenty-one members to take responsibility for decisions, a modified consensus approach has been adopted. This approach permits a group decision to be blocked by three or more members provided their reasons are linked to a relevant policy or principle. Invoking this procedure necessitates further group discussion prior to voting. This style of decision-making is felt to foster respect for all IRB members' opinions.[57] PWAs and HIV positive individuals work as CRI staff and are represented on the Board of Directors. A community advisory board of HIV positive individuals has also been established to discuss issues relating to research and treatment.[58]

CRI undertakes research sponsored by pharmaceutical companies as well as designing and conducting its own protocols. While government and academic researchers are focused on developing an HIV-specific cure, CRI is concerned to develop strategies concerning opportunistic infections.[59] Its testing strategies are also designed to reflect the needs of HIV/AIDS patients so that drugs are tested in conjunction with approved and non-approved medications.

CRI policy does not recognize a right on the part of potential subjects to enrolment in a particular protocol. In contrast to the inclusion criterion of "gravely ill patients" in NIH AIDS Treatment Centres, CRI trials include pre-AIDS and less sick AIDS patients. To ensure that research protocols are accessible to everyone, including groups which have been traditionally under-represented in research populations, namely IV drug users, Blacks, Hispanics, prisoners and women, IRB policy states that every effort will be made to ensure that:

-the demographics of patient groups enrolled in its research programs, when viewed over time, as a whole roughly reflect the demographics of the AIDS population in New York City;

-the exclusion criteria relate directly to the objectives of the study; in the case of exclusion criteria whose purpose is to ensure homogeneity of the study group, the criteria must lead to true homogeneity of the group, and it must be determined that this homogeneity is more beneficial for reaching the study objectives than having a heterogeneous study group reflective of the demographics of the AIDS population.[60]

In addition, CRI policy does not endorse protocols in which women and men of reproductive age are treated differently, unless there is a solid scientific basis for doing so. In assessing exclusion criteria concerning reproductive potential, including pregnancy, a higher value will not necessarily be placed on the potential risk to offspring than on the potential benefit to a trial participant. In reaching a decision, the availability of alternatives which pose a lesser risk to potential offspring will be taken into account. CRI policy also states that all trial participants must receive adequate information about potential adverse reproductive outcomes.[61]

In 1989, following a recommendation by the Presidential Commission on Human Immunodeficiency Virus Epidemic, the U.S. Congress approved a grant of 6 million dollars for community-based research programmes.[62] Financial support for community centres is also provided by organizations such as the American Foundation for AIDS Research (Am FAR). To date, twenty-four Am FAR supported centres have developed the capacity to undertake clinical trials. Of these ten have already undertaken trials.[63] A number of trials undertaken by community-based organizations have received FDA approval. Data from trials conducted by the San Francisco Community Consortium and CRI led to FDA approval of aerosolised pentamadine. A feature of this trial was that it did not involve a placebo.

The CRI model which seeks to involve PWAs in decision-making has profound implications for the researcher-subject relationship and for the form in which clinical trials are conducted. Its policy of broadened access is designed to include groups traditionally excluded by orthodox research protocols. The involvement of a patient's own doctor in clinical trials is likely to foster better communication which will encourage patient trust and co-operation. CRI's commitment to avoid conducting placebo-controlled trials wherever possible may encourage co-operation and avoid counter-productive practices such as pill sharing between treatment and control groups.

AUSTRALIAN CONTROLS GOVERNING NEW DRUG APPROVAL

New drug evaluation procedures

The regulation of prescription drugs in Australia is shared between Commonwealth and State Governments. Federal controls govern the importation of chemicals and drug marketing approval.[64] State legislation extends to the manufacture, sale and distribution of pharmaceuticals within State boundaries. To obtain marketing approval a sponsor must file a general marketing application containing information obtained during animal tests and clinical trials of its drug. The process of evaluation includes a stage calling for agreement between the Therapeutic Goods Administration (TGA) and a sponsor on the contents of a "Product Information" document. This document contains essential information concerning a drug's chemical identity, safety and efficacy, together with product information for prescribers. Assessment of quality, safety and efficacy is based upon a review of an application by the TGA and the Australian Drug Evaluation Committee (ADEC), a statutory committee composed of medical experts.[65] No weight is accorded to approvals granted by overseas authorities when reviewing Australian applications. Drug approval is a lengthy process in which the average time for granting marketing approval is approximately two years. In 1987, the Clinical Trials Exemption Scheme was established to expedite approval for the conduct of clinical trials. Critics of the scheme allege that it is a cumbersome and drawn-out process which acts as a strong disincentive to industry to undertake trials in Australia.[66]

The HIV/AIDS crisis has prompted renewed criticism of drug approval processes. According to one critic:

> In the absence of the political will to fast-track approval, a glacial regulatory system (taking, on average, 2 years from initial application to final approval or rejection) is clearly useless for people with HIV infection. It fails the underlying ethical principle of a drug regulatory system - to protect people - by affording no protection at all for the substantial number of people with HIV infection.[67]

Criticisms of current evaluation procedures together with recommendations for reform have been documented in a number of reports during the last decade. Many of the concerns which have not been addressed, are taken up in the report of a committee appointed by the Australian National Council on AIDS. Included in its recommendations is acceptance of marketing approval granted by recognized overseas regulatory authorities such as Britain and the United States.[68] Recommendations concerning the need to expedite patient access to experimental drugs are also contained in a recent report commissioned by the Minister for Aged, Family and Health Services.[69]

Individual patient usage scheme

Pursuant to the Therapeutic Goods Act 1989, an Individual Patient Usage (IPU) scheme provides compassionate access to experimental drugs for patients for whom conventional therapy is inappropriate or for whom no conventional therapy exists. Administrative guidelines restrict access to situations of clinical emergency, so that unapproved drugs cannot be accessed by patients with long-term fatal illnesses who are not critically ill.[70] Applications can only be made by medical practitioners who must monitor the effects of treatment and report any benefits or untoward effects. In the absence of a review system for IPU data, the scheme does not provide a useful means of generating safety and toxicity data.[71] In 1989, 20,000 IPU approvals were granted, prompting the criticism that what should be an exception is rapidly becoming a means of accessing treatments which are not being approved due to deficiencies in the system.[72] Although drugs accessed under IPU were initially supplied at cost, this policy was revised to incorporate "handling costs" because of an increasing use of the scheme as a means of obtaining expensive drugs. It appears that some companies are charging amounts which bear no relation to handling costs and which may yield a better return than a price approved under the Pharmaceutical Benefits Scheme, so that there is little incentive for a company to proceed with a marketing application.[73] This has prompted criticism that the scheme is providing a back-door method of marketing for some companies.[74] Because accessing such a system is dependent upon practitioner and patient initiative, the scheme has been criticized on the grounds that it gives rise to selective use.[75] The New South Wales AIDS Council recommended that urgent consideration be given to methods for expediting the approval of drugs for life-threatening illnesses, including HIV/AIDS. Suggested measures include developing mechanisms to provide early access to promising treatments.[76] A recent report by Professor Peter Baume recommends the establishment of a special scheme to enable access to experimental drugs, as well as drugs not approved in Australia but approved in comparable countries for persons suffering from a life-threatening condition.[77]

The special access scheme

A scheme for access to experimental drugs was established in January 1992, largely in response to recommendations contained in the Baume report.[78] The scheme replaces previous arrangements for individual patient use of unapproved drugs and grants access according to criteria based on an individual's health status. The scheme is dependent upon the co-operation of pharmaceutical manufacturers as a company is not required to supply a drug merely on the basis of its approval under the scheme. Category A patients are classified under the scheme as those who are terminally or seriously ill with a life-threatening condition. Such a condition is one from which death is reasonably likely to occur within a matter of months, or from which premature death is reasonably likely to occur in the absence of early treatment. A patient in this group may be prescribed any drug (except certain exempt drugs of abuse) by a treating doctor without prior approval from the TGA. The doctor must advise that the drug being sought is not approved for marketing and obtain written consent to the proposed treatment from the patient.[79] Category B patients are those suffering from a life-threatening condition, even if they are not critically ill. The drugs available to these patients are those acceptable under Category A which have been the subject of at least Phase 1 clinical trials, or which have an established history of safe use. Prior approval must be obtained by a treating practitioner from a delegate authorized under the Therapeutic Goods Act 1989.[80] Category C patients are those suffering from a serious, but not life-threatening illness. Drugs which are available to these patients are those acceptable under Category A which have been the subject of extensive clinical trials which have addressed safety and efficacy. Approval is sought from an authorized delegate, as in the case of Category B patients. If the drug has been approved in a designated country with a comparable regulatory system, the requirement to establish serious clinical need is reduced.[81] In the case of a drug which has been withdrawn from the Australian market, or which is unapproved, because of safety concerns, before an application will be considered, patients in Categories B and C must establish that all conventional therapy has been tried without success, or has resulted in unacceptable adverse reactions and that a serious clinical need exists.[82]

Individual import of unapproved drugs

The Therapeutic Goods Act 1989, permits importation into Australia of up to three months supply of a therapeutic substance for personal use.[83] Bulk imports or a single large import on behalf of a group are not permitted under the legislation. AIDS groups have criticized the restriction on bulk imports arguing that postage and other costs are prohibitive to all but a few.

Community trials network

In response to a report by the Australian National Council on AIDS Working Party on the Availability of HIV/AIDS Treatments, it is proposed to establish a Community AIDS Trials Network to promote and co-ordinate community-based clinical trials.[84]

THEORIES AND IDEAS CONCERNING DEVELOPMENTS IN REGULATORY POLICIES AND COMMUNITY-BASED RESEARCH INITIATIVES

In response to the AIDS crisis, regulatory authorities in both America and Australia have implemented policies designed to permit early access to experimental therapies. Community-based trial programmes tailored to the needs of PWAs have also been established in the United States. These initiatives obviously did not take place in a vacuum. Numerous ethical and legal issues which have been raised as a result of the

AIDS crisis have created a lively debate. In the following sections some of the ideas which are informing that debate are introduced.

Legal perspectives

Patient autonomy - defining limits

Some proponents of autonomy theory suggest that individuals have a right to decide what shall be done with their bodies, regardless of how irrational their decisions may appear to others. Because of the desperate situation of terminally ill patients, it is argued that as long as they are willing to accept risk of possible injury, no opportunity of a cure, including the use of unapproved therapies, should be denied them.[85] This libertarian view contrasts with the post-thalidomide stance of the consumer movement which welcomed FDA pre-marketing evaluation in the interests of consumer safety.

The consumer protection role of government in relation to experimental cancer has been endorsed by American courts. In the previously discussed Privitera and Rutherford decisions, patient choice was required to give way to government's role in protecting public health. These judicial decisions are compatible with the views of certain legal commentators who argue that libertarian views regarding freedom of choice do not satisfactorily address the possibility of terminally ill patients being harmed or exploited.[86] For this reason, governments are justified in denying access to drugs until acceptable margins of safety are established. Whilst not seeking to deny the importance of informed consent, George Annas argues that "the first and most important question is whether the experiment should be done at all". [87]

An unqualified interest in free choice presupposes adequate information on which to base such choice. In the present context, freedom to choose a course of treatment is possible only if available information is based on acceptable scientific studies, and there is an established regulatory mechanism for reviewing the safety and efficacy of potentially lethal or dangerous substances.[88] Others who agree with Annas also stress that patients must be aware of whether a treatment is proven, unproven or disproven as a prerequisite to free choice.[89] Patient autonomy and rights-based arguments should never be permitted to justify the use of disproven treatments.[90] Provided an acceptable margin of safety and effectiveness has been established by a regulatory authority, individuals should be free to choose a drug which may still be awaiting final marketing approval. The essence of this choice is that it is freely entered into and that the experimental status of the drug is clearly understood.[91]

Annas contends that apart from permitting the import of experimental therapies for personal use, the FDA has not deviated from its consumer protection role. Its broadened access initiatives are designed to streamline bureaucratic procedures rather than to substantively change drug evaluation rules.[92] Annas believes that this is an appropriate regulatory stance. Making unapproved therapies available outside of clinical trials is a cruel illusion that something is being done to combat death. He also suggests that if unapproved drugs are made readily available it will adversely affect recruitment into randomized clinical trials.[93] Instead, government must ensure adequate funds for clinical trials so that PWAs can be treated with safe and effective therapies.[94]

Gay rights / AIDS activist perspectives

Participatory decision-making

Expanded access to unapproved therapies and community-based research form part of a strategy designed to secure empowerment of AIDS-affected individuals through a process of community consultation.[95] Herbert Spiers describes community consultation in the context of AIDS as "a philosophical and ethical ideal - namely, the moral claim that persons affected by a disease have a right to participate in the process of finding cures and remedies for their illness".[96] The notion of participatory decision-making was an early concern of the consumer movement. As previously noted, the concept inspired the establishment of FDA advisory committees and subsequently human subject research ethics committees. In the hands of AIDS activists, consultation becomes a process rather than an event. It takes the form of an on-going dialogue which is institutionalized within the frameworks of clinical trials and the functioning of medical institutions.[97] Although the aim of consultation is empowerment of AIDS-affected individuals, the process must incorporate respect for scientific integrity in the conduct of clinical trials.[98] The notion of community is defined by Spiers as follows:

> "Community" ...represents the assembled interests of disparate persons and organizations seeking relief of the body's common affliction - AIDS/HIV disease. It also involves a collective self-awareness, as a community united against an established structure of power perceived to be inimical to the body politic of AIDS.[99]

As explained in the preceding chapter, the National Commission for the Protection of Human Subjects of Biomedical and Behavioral Research, identified respect for persons as one of three ethical principles underlying human subject research. The principle was interpreted as requiring that individuals should be treated as autonomous agents, capable of deciding what is in their own best interests. As a corollary, the commission determined that subjects must be adequately informed in order to decide whether or not to participate in clinical research. Informed consent provisions, both in Australia and America, require consultation between clinical researchers and subjects about specific aspects of a clinical trial.

Community consultation enhances participation in the development of protocols thereby facilitating the greater autonomy of research subjects.[100] Parallel track which was conceived by members of ACT UP, illustrates this point. Spiers describes this mechanism as having inaugurated a fundamental shift in scientific, bureaucratic and possibly bioethical paradigms. This is because it permits an active, on-going role for non-experts in the formulation of public policy relating to clinical trials and the accessibility of unapproved drugs.[101] In addition, by broadening the category of individuals eligible to obtain experimental substances, parallel track accords more closely with notions of distributive justice than do orthodox clinical trials which are subject to exclusion criteria.[102] Spiers suggests that "soft data" concerning symptoms caused or relieved by an experimental drug derived from parallel track can be used to supplement hard data obtained during orthodox clinical trials.[103]

Spiers describes the activities of CRI, along with ACT UP and the AIDS Treatment Registry, as "representing a demand for democratization in metascientific policy matters".[104] Moreover, CRI establishes an expanded form of participatory decision-making. By institutionalizing the process of consultation, it provides for regular input from representatives of the AIDS-affected community into the drug development process via committees. Whilst issues concerning the concept of community and the adequacy of representation remain, Spiers characterizes these initiatives as a significant marker in terms of community empowerment.[105]

Feminist perspectives

AIDS was initially identified as a disease which affected the male homosexual community. Gay rights and AIDS activists accused government and the scientific community of failing to respond quickly and adequately to the AIDS crisis because of homophobic attitudes which pervade society.[106] Nora Bell suggests that the anti-gay sentiments which followed detection of the AIDS virus overshadowed the plight of women with AIDS.[107] Lacking a natural community like the gay community, she believes that women with AIDS are the most disadvantaged group in American society.[108] Whilst pointing out that she does not consider the gay community in any way to blame, Bell contends that women have also been disadvantaged by attempts to combat homophobia. In particular, she points to early policy initiatives which focused on privacy issues. Whilst acknowledging the importance of these issues, she claims that they had a detrimental effect on other public health measures such as partner notification and contact tracing. As a result, women and men were deprived of vital information.[109] Carol Levine argues that despite the fact that the number of reported cases of infected women is increasing, the initial characterization of AIDS as a disease affecting gay white males or black and hispanic male drug users, continues to impede the development of suitable educational and health care programmes for women, including access to clinical trials of promising new drugs.[110]

Gay rights and AIDS activists, bioethicists and members of the medical profession have recognized that the principle of equitable access should govern the selection of trial populations.[111] According to Carol Levine, despite the prevalence of AIDS-infected women and the possibility that they may need different treatment, drug trials to date have involved mostly male subjects.[112] The success of gay rights and AIDS activists in affecting changes in regulatory policies regarding access to experimental drugs has prompted womens' and ethnic minority groups in the United States, to demand access to clinical trials for HIV experimental drugs. Exclusion from clinical trials is no longer accepted as a consumer protection measure by these groups. Instead, it is perceived as an issue involving principles of equity and equal opportunity. In response to the efforts of womens' organizations, NIH has recently revised its policy to provide that women shall be included in biomedical research studies, unless inclusion is inappropriate, or a compelling justification for exclusion exists.[113] A similar policy has also been published by NIH regarding the inclusion of minorities.[114] The importance of these policy initiatives is that they seek to ensure a more equitable selection of subjects "who will undertake the risks and share in the benefits of research".[115]

OVERVIEW

During the sixties, publicity concerning unethical research practices and side-effects caused by certain drugs helped to create public acceptance of regulatory controls to protect research participants. Procedural safeguards in both the United States and Australia incorporate requirements governing participants' consent and the functions of ethical review committees. While partly concerned with the autonomy of research participants, the major objective of regulatory policy was to avoid harm to or the exploitation of research populations. These initiatives had a significant impact on the research establishment which previously had exercised decision-making powers undisturbed by outside scrutiny.

During the eighties, as a result of the AIDS crisis, regulatory systems in the United States and Australia came under increasing pressure from AIDS activists to make unapproved drugs rapidly available to PWAs. They also made demands for participatory decision-making in relation to the development of clinical trial protocols and in all aspects of policies concerning AIDS-affected individuals. Dissatisfaction with randomized clinical trials, in particular the use of placebos and exclusion criteria which discriminated against women, drug users and ethnic minorities, led to the establishment of community-based trials programmes in the United States. We now turn to assess these regulatory changes and community-based initiatives.

Expanded access

The demands of AIDS and cancer sufferers for access to unapproved drugs directly challenges the consumer protection role of regulatory authorities. Due to the fatal nature of their diseases, many of these individuals are willing to accept the possibility of risk of injury from unapproved substances. These demands raise questions concerning the limits of patient autonomy vis à vis the role of government as protector of public health and safety. Government policy should not endorse unqualified individual freedom of choice. Because governments have been entrusted with a mandate to protect the public health and safety, they are justified in setting limits in regard to those risks which individuals are entitled to take. For this reason, a waiving of all standards in the case of drugs imported for personal use is hard to justify. A major challenge to policy makers in this area is to maintain a balance between the long-term goals of science and the immediate needs and demands of terminally ill individuals. Researchers and government officials in the United States and Australia have recognized a need to speed up the process of drug approval and to increase patient access. At the same time, there is an awareness of a need to preserve clinical testing in order to accumulate data and scientific knowledge for the benefit of future patients.

The deadly nature of HIV/AIDS must not allow safety standards to be compromised. Understandably there is enthusiasm amongst HIV/AIDS groups for the introduction a system of parallel track in Australia.[116] A recent conference in the United States sponsored by the Institute of Medicine highlights some issues which need to be addressed. First, in conventional clinical trials, protocols must be approved by an IRB. It appears that such an arrangement might be impractical for parallel track protocols. This is because many community physicians who wish to participate would not have access to an IRB. In addition, the time required to provide information to such a body would prevent rapid dissemination of drugs to desperately ill patients. In order to address this problem, it has been proposed that a National panel should be established to provide continuing ethical review of all parallel track protocols.[117] Second, recent experience with open access to the drug ddi has caused concern amongst researchers that the system will result in a decrease in participation in clinical trials.[118] Third, the ultimate importance of data obtained from expanded access remains uncertain.[119] Fourth, experience with treatment INDs and parallel track indicates that the ability of physicians to assess a treatment is adversely affected by the long delays between the initial publicity about a new drug and the publication of trial data in peer-reviewed journals. Consequently, there is a need to develop mechanisms which will enable data to be rapidly reviewed and transmitted to physicians and their patients to facilitate informed choice.[120]

The principle of equitable access

The AIDS crisis has highlighted the need to ensure that the principle of equitable access governs the selection of research populations for clinical trials. The principle demands that vulnerable groups are not systematically included because of their ready availability, their compromised position, or their manipulability, rather than for their relevance to the problem being studied. It also requires that groups are not unfairly excluded from research studies. Although TGA guidelines stipulate that researchers should employ the principle in the selection of research subjects, there is no indication as to how this policy is to be interpreted or implemented with respect to women or ethnic minorities.[121] As we have seen, post-thalidomide the principle has been interpreted in terms of protecting vulnerable research populations. Undoubtedly regulatory policy must ensure that especially vulnerable individuals are not selected as participants in trials simply as a matter of scientific expediency and that their inclusion is in their own interests.[122] At the same time, there is a need for additional guidelines along the lines of NIH initiatives which will ensure that women and ethnic minorities are given an equal opportunity to participate in appropriate clinical trials.[123] The principle of equal access is not the sole concern of clinical researchers. NHMRC and TGA guidelines should also require that research ethics committees examine research protocols to ensure that the principle has been observed in appropriate circumstances in the selection of research subjects.

Participatory decision-making

A fundamental characteristic of democratic decision-making is that all affected parties, or their duly appointed representatives, parties should participate. This principle, which is inherent in the notion of informed consent, is also incorporated within the concept of the FDA advisory committee system and research ethics committees. AIDS activists argue that the principle requires that representatives of PWAs are included in policy, advisory and research ethics committees.[124] Whilst these demands are unobjectionable, the real difficulty lies in selecting representatives of PWAs. Whilst defining a group in terms of illness may be acceptable for medical purposes, it is not adequate as a political concept as it obscures further distinctions including race and gender. The problems of women with AIDS are undeniably different from those of men afflicted with the AIDS virus. In the case of AIDS, further differences arise based on IV drug use, age, and ethnicity. The concept of an "AIDS community" is politically unacceptable as it fails to take account of the particular needs of these various groups.

Community research initiatives

The community-based trials initiative raises a number of important issues, one of which is the involvement of local doctors as investigators. For those who believe that research is a joint venture, the use of local doctors may be viewed as a factor encouraging trust between patient and physician. For others, it will be seen as dangerously blurring the boundaries between treatment and research and creating conflicts of interest for the physician-investigators. Because of the different objectives of the clinical and research relationships, participants must be informed as to whether a doctor is acting solely as an investigator or as a physician-investigator.[125]

The AIDS crisis illustrates the effectiveness of grass roots organizations in affecting significant policy changes. It also illustrates the possibility for collaborative decision-making between government, medical researchers and gay rights and AIDS activists. An immediate challenge is to ensure that the voices of women, children, drug users, aboriginal people and other ethnic minorities are also included in the on-going dialogue.

Notes

1. Wolfe S., Public Citizen Health Research Group, Statement on the Export of Unapproved Drugs before the Committee on Labor and Human Resources, U.S. Senate, Washington D.C. June 5, 1985.
2. Expanding Access to Investigational Therapies for HIV Infection and AIDS. The Institute of Medicine's Roundtable for the Development of Drugs and Vaccines Against AIDS, March 12-13, 1990, National Academy Press Washington D.C.1991, 8-9. (Hereinafter referred to as Expanding Access to Investigational Therapies)
3. Levine C., Neveloff Dubler N. and Levine R., Building a New Consensus: Ethical Principles and Policies for Clinical Research on HIV/AIDS. 13 IRB: A Review of Human Subjects Research 1991, 1,4.
4. Vogel D., AIDS and the politics of drug lag. 96 The Public Interest. 1989, 73, 75.
5. The terms 'unconventional' and 'unorthodox' are sometimes used interchangeably to describe treatments falling outside the bounds of mainstream medicine. These terms refer to drugs which have not been subject to regulatory review for safety and effectiveness. 'Disproven therapy' refers to therapies, which as a result of regulatory review have been found to be of little or no therapeutic value. Schwartz R.D. and Burke R.L., Legal Constraints on the Availability of Unorthodox Cancer Treatments: Consumer Protection View. Contract report for the Office of Technology Assessment, U.S.Congress Washington D.C. April, 1988, 135.
6. U.S. Congress, Office of Technology Assessment, Unconventional Cancer Treatments, OTA-H-405 (Washington, DC: U.S.Government Printing Office, September 1990) 3. (Hereinafter referred to as OTA Unconventional Cancer Treatments.)
7. Houston G.R., Repression and Reform in the Evaluation of Alternative Cancer Therapies. Project Cure, Washington D.C. 1989,1.
8. OTA Unconventional Cancer Treatments, op.cit. 202.
9. Houston, op.cit. 52. Medical practitioners are subject to the provisions of state licencing statutes and the common law.
10. Freedman B., Nonvalidated Therapies and HIV Disease. 19 Hastings Center Report 1989 14, 15.
11. OTA Unconventional Cancer Treatments, op.cit. 3.
12. Id.228.
13. Id.10-11.
14. Id.3.
15. Hearings on Quackery before the Select Committee on Aging of the House, 98th Cong. 2nd.Sess, 240 (May 31, 1984) as cited in Schwartz and Burke op.cit. 25, 27.
16. Houston, op.cit. 12.
17. Id.16-7.
18. Id.14.
19. Id.37.

20. Moertel et al., A Clinical Trial of Amygdalin (Laetrile) in the Treatment of Human Cancer.306 New England Journal of Medicine 1982, 201; U.S. Congress, Office of Technology Assessment, OTA Unconventional Cancer Treatments, 21-22.
21. OTA Unconventional Cancer Treatments, op.cit. 22.
22. Id.24-6.
23. The right of privacy includes freedom of an individual to make fundamental choices involving the individual, his or her family and others, except where the choice occasions harm. The U.S. Supreme Court has created zones of privacy in a number of health-related areas including contraception, abortion, and medical decision-making, including the right to refuse medical treatment. U.S. Congress, Office of Technology Assessment, Unconventional Cancer Treatments, OTA- H-405 (Washington D.C. Government Printing Office, 1990, 198 n.2.
24. The court reasoned that the decisions falling within a right of privacy included matters relating to marriage, procreation, contraception and other family related issues but did not include medical treatment.
25. People v Privitera 23 Cal.3d 697, 153 Cal.Rptr.431, 591 P 2d 919 (1979).
26. United States v Rutherford, 442 U.S. 544, (1979)
27. Id. at 555.
28. Id. at 555-6.
29. Rutherford v United States 616 F.2d 455 (10th Cir.1980) at 457.
30. Tribe L., American Constitutional Law 1978, 564-75, as cited in Schwartz and Burke, op.cit. 124.
31. Schwartz and Burke, op.cit. 124.
32. Id.124-5.
33. Schneider v Revici et al., (1V. No.83-8035) D.Ct.S.D. N.Y., December 2,1985.
34. Schneider v Revici   817 F.2d 987 (2nd.Cir.1987) as cited in OTA Unconventional Cancer Treatments, op.cit. 200.
35. Edgar H. and Rothman D., New Rules for New Drugs: The Challenge of AIDS to the Regulatory Process. 68 Milbank Quarterly, Suppl.1.1990, 123.
36. A number of informal ways of expanding access were developed by the FDA. Compassionate use IND, open label safety studies and Group C cancer drug INDs were referred to above.
37. 21 CFR s.312.34 (1989); OTA Unconventional Cancer Treatments, op.cit. 203.
38. Kessler D., The Regulation of Investigational Drugs. 320 New England Journal of Medicine 1989, 284.
39. Marlin M., Treatment INDs: A faster Route To Drug Approval? 39 The American University Law Review 1989, 171, 185-6.
40. Kessler, op.cit. 284.
41. Marlin, op.cit. 186.
42. 52 Fed.Reg.19,465, 19,473 (1987) as cited in Annas G., Faith (Healing), Hope and Charity at the FDA: The Politics of AIDS Drug Trials. 34 Villanova Law Review 1989, 771, 782 n.40.
43. Up to March 1990, the FDA had approved eighteen treatment INDs for a number of conditions including AIDS.

44. Report of the Presidential Commission on the Human Immunodeficiency Virus Epidemic 50 (1988) as cited in Annas, op.cit. 782, n.39.
45. Kessler, op.cit. 285.
46. Annas, op.cit. 783.
47. Expanding Access to Investigational Therapies, op.cit. 13-14.
48. Spiers H., Community Consultation and AIDS Clinical Trials: 13 IRB: A Review of Human Subjects Research 1991, (Part 2) 3; Treatment Agenda 1990, ACT UP/ New York. VI International Conference on AIDS San Francisco, June 1990, 21.
49. Expanding Access to Investigational Therapies, op.cit. 16.
50. Levine, Neveloff Dubler and Levine, op.cit. 5.
51. Expanding Access to Investigational Therapies, op.cit. 18.
52. Id.17-18.
53. Expanding Access to Investigational Therapies, op.cit. 11-12.
54. Ibid.
55. Merton V., Community-Based AIDS Research. 14 Evaluation Review 1990, 502.
56. Id.502-4.
57. Id.506.
58. Spiers, op.cit. Part 2, 2.
59. Deaths are occurring not because of AIDS per se, but as a result of cancers, pneumonia and chronic infections that cannot be controlled once the body's immune system breaks down. Spiers op.cit. Part 2, 1.
60. Merton, op.cit. 503, 516-7.
61. Id.521.
62. Id.505.
63. Am FAR Annual Report 1989-90, 8.
64. The Therapeutic Goods Act 1989 is intended to provide a system of uniform control over therapeutic goods in Australia. The Act, together with pursuant regulations, forms the legislative basis for the regulation of clinical trials.
65. Since the role of ADEC is a purely advisory one, there is no statutory obligation requiring the Minister, or his delegate, to accept the committee's advice. In practice however, its advice is invariably accepted. For criticism of current evaluation procedures see, A Question of Balance - Report on the future of Drug Evaluation in Australia. Australian Government Publishing Service, 1991, Chapter 6 (Hereinafter referred to as Report on the future of Drug Evaluation in Australia).
66. Trialing Approval and Marketing of Treatments and Therapies for HIV/AIDS and Related Illnesses In Australia. AIDS Council of New South Wales 1990 para.3.5.3. (Hereinafter referred to as Trailing Approval and Marketing of Treatments and Therapies for HIV/AIDS); Report on the future of Drug Evaluation in Australia, op.cit. 48-52.
67. Kerans P., AZT, Early Intervention and Drug Regulation. 4 National AIDS Bulletin 1990, as cited in Trialing Approval and Marketing of Treatments and Therapies for HIV/AIDS, op.cit. para.3.5.
68. Report of the Australian National Council on AIDS, Working Party on the Availability of HIV/AIDS Treatments, December 1990.

69. Report on the future of Drug Evaluation in Australia, op.cit.
70. Id.123-4, 129.
71. Trialing Approval and Marketing of Treatments and Therapies for HIV/AIDS para.3.6.4.
72. Id.para.3.6.3.
73. The scheme is one of partial federal subsidy for prescription drugs under which the consumer contributes a small proportion of a drug included in the scheme, the balance being paid by the government. The benefit is available only in respect of listed drugs. Decisions as to listing are taken by the Minister for Health on the advice of the Pharmaceutical Benefits Advisory Committee.
74. Trailing Approval and Marketing of Treatments and Therapies for HIV/AIDS. para. 3.6.7.
75. Id. para.3.6.9.
76. Id. para.3.5.5.6.
77. Report of the future of Drug Evaluation in Australia, op.cit. Chapter 9.
78. Access To Unapproved Drugs Via The Special Access Scheme (SAS). Therapeutic Goods Administration, 1 January, 1992.
79. Id.2.
80. Id.3.
81. Id.4
82. Id.5.
83. Therapeutic Goods Act 1989, s.18. For a recent decision permitting the import of laetrile by a cancer patient see Calleja v The Secretary to The Department of Community Services and Health. Federal Court of Western Australia, 15 November, 1990.
84. For recent recommendations concerning the introduction of community-based trails in Australia see Trialing Approval and Marketing of Treatments and Therapies for HIV/AIDS, op.cit. para.2.11 -2.15
85. Annas, op.cit. 777,n.21., citing Kramer L., Reports From The Holocaust 142 1989.("AIDS sufferers, who have nothing to lose, are more than willing to be guinea pigs".)
86. Id.783.
87. Id.778, n.22 citing Fletcher., The Evolution of the Ethics of Informed Consent, in Research Ethics 211 (K. Berg and K.Tranoy eds 1983).
88. Id.792; Schwartz and Burke, op.cit. 127
89. Schwartz and Burke, op.cit. 127.
90. Ibid.
91. Id.132-3.
92. Annas, op.cit. 793.
93. Id.786.
94. Id.796.
95. Spiers op.cit. parts 1-3.
96. Spiers, op.cit. part 1, 8.
97. Ibid.
98. Spiers, op.cit. part 3, 7. Like the concept of community, Spiers notes that the concept of empowerment is also a difficult one. Id.3.
99. Spiers, op.cit. part 1, 8.

100. Spiers, op.cit. part 3, 4.
101. Spiers, op.cit. part, 2, 3.
102. Spiers, op.cit. part 2, 3.
103. Ibid.
104. Spiers, op.cit. part 3, 4. The activities of the AIDS Treatment Registry are described in part 2 of Spier's article.
105. Id.3-7.
106. Spiers, op.cit. part 1,8.
107. Bell N.K., Women and AIDS; Too Little, Too Late? in Feminist Perspectives in Medical Ethics. Holmes H.B. and Purdy L.M.(eds). Indiana University Press 1992, 46, 49-50.
108. Id.51, 59.
109. Id.51.
110. Levine C., Women and HIV/ AIDS Research: The Barriers to Equity. 13 IRB - A Review of Human Subjects Research 1991, 18.
111. Spiers, op.cit. part 2,3; Macklin R. and Friedland G., AIDS Research: The Ethics of Clinical Trials 14 Law, Medicine and Health Care 273, 276; Levine, Neveloff Dubler and Levine, op.cit. 14-17.
112. Levine, op.cit. 18.
113. NIH Guide, Vol.2D, 8 February, 1991.
114. NIH Guide, 25 September, 1987.
115. Levine, op.cit. 22.
116. Trialing, Approval and Marketing of Treatments and Therapies for HIV/AIDS op.cit. para.2.11.23.
117. Expanding Access to Experimental Therapies, op.cit. 18.
118. Id.31-2.
119. Id.41-2.
120. Id.21-2.
121. TGA Guidelines for Good Clinical Research Practice (GCRP) in Australia 1991 2.1.6.
122. Levine, Neveloff Dubler and Levine, op.cit. 2. The authors suggest that vulnerable individuals require special consideration in the design and implementation of clinical trials.
123. Trailing Approval and Marketing of Treatments and Therapies for HIV/AIDS, op.cit. rec.2.6.
124. Spiers, op.cit. part 1, 8, part 3, 5; Trailing Approval and Marketing of Treatments and Therapies for HIV/AIDS, op.cit. recs. 4.4, 6.11.
125. Levine, Neveloff Dubler and Levine, op.cit. 13.

6 Patients as Decision-Makers: A Postscript

The starting point of this narrative is the sixties - an era in which rights rhetoric and anti-authoritarian sentiments shaped social consciousness and political activity. Interest groups and the newly-emerging field of bioethics generated a public discourse throughout the following decades which signalled the decline of medical paternalism. No longer prepared to be "seen and not heard", patients began demanding to be included in medical decision-making. The evolution of ideas as generators of social change and their effect on legal and voluntary standards governing medical practice is a central theme of this work. A fascinating, inter-connected issue is how and why these ideas and theories originated. Rights consciousness, kindled by the American civil rights movement, shaped the activities of interest groups. Similar rights movements subsequently emerged in Australia. But this is only part of our story. There were also significant changes in health care delivery and an increasing use of medical technology in both countries. These factors undoubtedly contributed to feelings of patient isolation and anonymity. Dramatic incidents, including the thalidomide drug tragedy, the plight of Karen Ann Quinlan and the AIDS crisis, prompted scholars and interest groups to devise theories and methods for empowering patients, with particular regard to decision-making processes. Interestingly, their contributions prompted different responses from lawmakers in each of the areas canvassed in this book.

The first aspect of clinical decision-making to be explored concerned consent to medical treatment. We have seen that largely as a result of the thalidomide disaster, the consumer movement began demanding a right to information as a necessary pre-requisite to informed choice. Consumer organizations drew attention to inequalities in education and expertise between practitioners and patients. In addition, structural deficiencies within the health care system, including time constraints, team care and lack of interpreter services, were identified as significant barriers to imparting information to patients. Feminists were quick to criticize a health care system in which women's needs were either ignored or interpreted from a male perspective. In common with certain legal and bioethical views, radical feminists argued that responsibility to decide for oneself is a fundamental liberty. Applied in a medical context, an autonomy perspective requires doctors to facilitate decision-making by providing expert information, whilst ultimate decision-making authority rests with the patient. Withholding information from patients, regardless of whether it is deemed in their best interests, is perceived as unjustified paternalism. Others, including doctors and bioethicists, rejected paternalistic and patient autonomy models of decision-making preferring to characterize decision-making as a joint enterprise. By fostering a continuing dialogue, it was argued that some of the social, psychological, and structural impediments to communication could be overcome.

As these various theories and ideas emerged depicting a new role for patients in medical decision-making, American and Australian courts were developing disclosure standards within the framework of negligence law. The American civil rights movement gave birth to a new rights consciousness which ultimately shaped the law concerning the treatment of black Americans and other minority groups. Rights rhetoric permeated other areas, including the clinical relationship. In response to patients demands for a right to information, American courts developed the doctrine of informed consent culminating in the case Canterbury v Spence. Its rejection of professional judgement in determining the standard of care was heralded as a triumph for patients' rights. The impact of the judgement in this respect was nevertheless overshadowed by the strictures of negligence law concerning the limits of disclosure and causation. Shortly afterwards, the role of the American courts in defining patients' decision-making rights concerning consent to treatment was effectively curtailed by legislation.

In contrast to the ready adoption of rights rhetoric by American judges, Australian judges, with a few notable exceptions, have failed to incorporate theories of patient autonomy and rights into the law of information disclosure. As previously noted, the confines of negligence law prevented Australian and American courts adopting a full-blown theory of patient autonomy as developed by legal, bioethical and feminist scholars. Proceeding from a duty perspective, the main focus of the Australian common law is on risk disclosure. Professional medical opinion continues to play a central role in establishing what constitutes acceptable medical conduct, despite the fact that it is ultimately a question of law. Thus far, Australian case law has remained largely unaffected by public discourse about patients as decision-makers. This is consistent with judicial attitudes in the area of consumer transactions where it has fallen to State and Federal parliaments to establish consumer rights by way of statutory standards. Confined to determining particular disputes, courts are not well-suited to embarking on far-reaching enquiries concerning political, social and psychological dimensions of patient-doctor communication and decision-making. Restrictive procedural rules and the cost of litigation keep courts beyond the reach of the vast majority of aggrieved patients. Consequently, there are limited opportunities for courts to be instruments of social change in an Australian context. Nevertheless, activities of Law Reform Commissions have compensated for reduced judicial involvement in this area of patient decision-making. Whilst courts have not been quick to recognize the doctrine of informed consent, the concept was incorporated in the title and introductory paragraph of a joint Law Reform Commissions' discussion paper.

In accordance with the Commissions' recommendations, an NHMRC working party, comprising professional and lay members, has published draft voluntary guidelines on decision-making.   Acknowledging that, in accordance with community expectations, individuals are entitled to make their own decisions, the guidelines seek to encourage joint decision-making. In addition to specifying the type of information to be disclosed, attention is paid to the method of conveying information to ensure patient comprehension and participation. Information is required to be provided in a form and manner appropriate to the patient's circumstances, personality, expectations, fears, beliefs, values and cultural background. This degree of attention to individual needs and characteristics is closer to a subjective ethics of care approach rather than to an objective reasonable patient standard at common law. By blending bioethical, medical, feminist and consumer views, the guidelines represent an innovative approach to clinical decision-making. It is clear that if legislation is enacted enabling the guidelines to be admissible as evidence in judicial proceedings, they will undoubtedly influence the development of common law standards. The guidelines also provide a code of conduct which can be used as a basis for educating patient and practitioners. However, a public education campaign will be necessary to inform patients of their rights and responsibilities as decision-makers.

The second aspect of clinical decision-making to be discussed concerned refusal of medical treatment. In this area, American courts are actively involved in defining patients' decision-making rights. At the same time, there has been considerable legislative activity at State and Federal levels concerning the making of advance directives. Suggested reasons for resort to the courts include the large numbers of people dying in institutions which makes death a public event. There is also a great deal of uncertainty and fear on the part of health care providers regarding their legal liability in the event of treatment termination. In addition, there has not been an ousting of judicial determination in this area as occurred in relation to consent to treatment following the explosion of malpractice litigation. Consistent with their approach concerning consent to treatment, American judges have characterized the right to refuse medical treatment as a necessary element of an individual's right of self-determination. In some instances, they have also recognized a right of privacy as a basis for treatment refusal. However, a right of refusal is not absolute and must be considered together with a number of relevant State interests.

Whilst American courts readily established a right to refuse treatment in the case of competent patients, defining rights for incompetent patients has proved a more difficult task. In the Quinlan case, the court adopted a form of substituted judgement allowing guardian and family to decide on Quinlan's behalf, subject to consultation with medical staff and the hospital ethics committee. In the Conroy case, the court indicated that a right of self-determination may properly be exercised by a surrogate decision-maker on behalf of an incompetent patient, provided a subjective test, or one of two best interests tests, is satisfied. What constitutes acceptable evidence of an incompetent patient's wishes may differ as between jurisdictions. Recently, the United States Supreme Court confirmed in the Cruzan case that a State may legitimately require that an intention to refuse treatment in the case of incompetent patients must be established by clear and convincing evidence. In the Quinlan, Conroy and Cruzan cases, the courts were attempting to ascertain the wishes of once-competent patients. The more difficult cases are those involving never-competent patients. In the

Saikewicz case, the court adopted a substituted judgement test on the grounds that it respected Saikewicz's autonomy. In the Storar case, the court implicitly rejected this approach on the grounds that as Storar had never been competent, it would be unrealistic to attempt to determine what he would have chosen, if competent. Instead, the court chose to treat Storar as an infant so that life-saving treatment could not be refused on his behalf by parents or guardians.

Involvement of the courts in this area of decision-making has not been greeted with great enthusiasm by the United States President's Commission for the Study of Ethical Problems in Medicine and Biomedical and Behavioral Research. This Commission suggested that routine resort to the judicial system should not be encouraged. Similarly, a majority of the commentators included in Chapter Three recommend judicial intervention only as a last resort. Some argue that judicial emphasis on self-determination in the case of incompetent patients is misplaced and likely to result in their abandonment. Further, because judicial resolution fails to deal with political and social dimensions of treatment refusal, it excludes consideration of the needs of the terminally ill for a caring and compassionate environment. For those who espouse an ethics of care, legal rules are felt to be too impersonal. An emphasis on relationships is preferred because it allows personal particulars to be taken into account which might otherwise be excluded by the application of objective legal standards.

In contrast to the American situation, Australian courts are resorted to relatively infrequently in the area of treatment refusal. To date, legislation enabling individuals to make advance directives has been enacted in two Australian States. After considering American case law and noting the diverse outcomes, a specially-appointed Victorian government committee opted for a legislative, as opposed to a common law, approach. The resulting Victorian Medical Treatment Act 1988, contains an unqualified endorsement of a patient's right to refuse medical treatment. Modelled on the recommendations contained in the President's Commission report **Foregoing Life-Sustaining Treatment,** the legislation vests decision-making in patients, their duly-appointed representatives and doctors. In these circumstances, resort to the courts is likely to be a relatively rare event. In the case of incompetent patients, flexible procedural safeguards enable duly-appointed surrogate decision-makers to employ either a best interest test or to exercise a substituted judgement. In either case, the adoption of a criterion of reasonableness, coupled with lay as opposed to legal interpretation, is likely to yield a broad range of interpretations and a reliance on subjective information consistent with an ethics of care approach.

The legislation is designed to clarify patients' decision-making rights by making it an offence to commence or continue treatment once a refusal certificate has been signed. The legislation seeks to ensure that patients will not be abandoned to their autonomy as a result of deciding not to continue treatment by specifically excluding palliative care from the definition of medical treatment. Whilst this legislation goes a long way towards clarifying patients' rights to refuse treatment, legal recognition of rights will be inadequate unless those rights are supported by measures to ensure their implementation. Education campaigns will be necessary to advise people of the available options, including the appointment of surrogate decision-makers. Most importantly, it should be possible for terminally ill and dying patients to spend their last days in a caring and compassionate environment, by virtue of an expanded hospice programme. Only when decision-making includes such an option will the most vulnerable members of our society be offered a meaningful choice which will permit death with dignity.

Exploration of the research relationship also revealed changes in the decision-making role of research subjects. In both Australia and America, courts have not been involved in standard setting. Instead, measures have been implemented by regulatory authorities in response to publicity concerning unethical experimentation. To safeguard the interests of research subjects, the concept of informed consent and independent scrutiny of research by ethics committees were incorporated into American administrative regulations and Australian voluntary standards.

During the seventies, bioethicists, feminists and others developed theories of patient self-determination as a necessary counter-balance to medical paternalism. American, and to a lesser extent Australian, courts incorporated the concept of patient autonomy into existing principles of negligence law. It was also taken up by a United States National Commission charged with identifying ethical principles which should govern human subject research. The Commission stated that respect for persons required that individuals should be treated as autonomous agents. Further, that research subjects must be adequately informed so that they can freely decide whether to participate in experimentation. The importance which the Commission attached to patient autonomy was also reflected in its adoption of a reasonable person standard of disclosure for the purposes of obtaining informed consent. At the same time, concern for research subjects' welfare and safety is evident in the Commission's statement on the selection of research populations. These selection procedures were included to prevent the systematic selection of vulnerable groups - a concern also shared by certain feminists and moral theologians.

Throughout the sixties, seventies and into the eighties, the concept of self-determination for research subjects was not developed to the same extent as it was in a clinical context. This was due largely to safety concerns, shared by government and public alike, which followed in the wake of publicity concerning unethical experimentation. Certainly, there were instances of cancer patients challenging the concept by seeking access to unapproved therapies via the American courts. However, it was not until the AIDS crisis that concepts of rights and autonomy had a significant impact on human subject research regulation in Australia and the United States.

In Australia, there has been no equivalent body to the American National Commission which has identified ethical standards for research. Lacking the detail of the American regulations, NHMRC guidelines on informed consent fail to adequately safeguard research subjects' interests. Recently, the TGA has issued informed consent guidelines which are closely modelled on the American regulations. As a result, Australian guidelines now reflect the National Commission's emphasis on patient autonomy.

The role of research ethics committees has also attracted a good deal of public interest throughout the last two decades. The basic responsibility of these bodies is to ensure that research subjects are protected from harm during the conduct of clinical trials. The rationale for the inclusion of lay representatives on these bodies is that it enables research to be evaluated according to the community's sense of proper conduct. Public debate on the role and function of ethics committees has included issues of adequacy of representation of various interest groups and the dominance of scientific members over lay representatives. These issues are common to all forms of participatory decision-making. Recently, the issue of representation has been debated in relation to community consultation processes in the context of AIDS.

Changes in American and Australian regulatory policy have resulted in broader access to unapproved drugs for certain classes of patients. These initiatives in drug regulatory policy permit a new form of decision-making which vests seriously-ill individuals with greater responsibility to make decisions regarding the drugs they take. The changes were prompted by the demands of gay rights and AIDS activists for patient autonomy and a right of access to unapproved therapies. Expanded access policies represent a move away from regulatory paternalism towards autonomous decision-making. Nevertheless, regulatory authorities in both Australia and the United States require safety to be established for drugs available under expanded access schemes. Interestingly, personal use importation regulations in both countries represent a clear departure from regulatory policy in this respect.

The AIDS crisis has also prompted demands for a greater degree of participatory decision-making by AIDS-affected individuals. AIDS activists and organizations argue that a process of community consultation is essential to ensure an on-going institutionalized dialogue which includes the "AIDS community" in the formulation of AIDS policies. These groups urge that such a process is necessary both to provide expanded access and to ensure equitable selection of research subjects. The success of gay rights groups and AIDS activists and organizations in securing changes in regulatory policies regarding access to experimental drugs has prompted women's and ethnic minority groups in the United States to demand to be included in clinical trials. Their demands, which have caused NIH to revise its policies, represent an important challenge to the principles of justice and equitable access as the exclusion of certain groups from trial populations is no longer accepted as a consumer protection measure. Instead, it is regarded as unjustifiable discrimination. As women are infected by the AIDS virus in increasing numbers, feminists argue that AIDS-related debate and policies must take account of gender. For them, the concept of an AIDS community is politically unacceptable as it fails to take sufficient account of the needs of diverse groups, including women.

In exploring clinical and research decision-making in Australia and the United States we identified social movements which reject a paternalistic view of patients as passive recipients of medical treatment. We glimpsed the gradual absorption of some of their ideas into legal and voluntary standards affecting decision-making processes. We also discovered a discernible pattern of American legal concepts and regulatory models forming the basis of Australian voluntary and legislative guidelines.

During the last three decades, patients, as decision-makers, have come a long way. Nevertheless, traditional problems associated with participatory decision-making remain. Representative decision-making is dependent upon equitable access, yet it is clear that certain groups are more politically adept than others, and hence more skilled at presenting their point of view and ensuring its acceptance. The notion of 'representative' is also fraught with difficulties. This is because the broad spectrum of views within interest groups makes it extremely difficult to identify a representative stance on a particular issue. These limitations do not negate the value of representative decision-making. Rather, they highlight the need to develop mechanisms and procedures which will ensure a broad canvassing of views on individual issues. Each of the social movements explored in this book developed its own rights agenda. However, it is clear that legal recognition of rights alone is rarely adequate. Rights are not isolated legal entitlements - they exist within political and social contexts. In most instances, their successful implementation requires the identification of additional measures. These will undoubtedly necessitate increased expenditures, or a re-allocation of health funds. In either case, hard political choices will be necessary.

As we enter the nineties, it seems likely that public debate about health needs and access to health care will be increasingly subject to economic considerations. Both in the United States and Australia the imposition of economic constraints on individual choice in health matters is already being foreshadowed. In response, the groups most likely to be affected - the elderly, women and minorities - have begun to register their concerns. The prospect of a narrow economics-dominated bioethics agenda is a daunting one which threatens the hard-fought for gains of the last decade. Yet despite the current economic doom and gloom there is still reason to be optimistic. The AIDS crisis demonstrates the difficulty of maintaining a balance between individual demands and those which the community is prepared to recognize. At the same time, it has shown us that achieving such a balance is both possible and necessary for achieving community health in its broadest sense.

147

Index

149

153